PHILIP'S

STREETS

Edinburgh

C000293316

First published 2003 by

Philip's, a division of
Octopus Publishing Group Ltd
2–4 Heron Quays
London E14 4JP

First edition 2003
First impression 2003

ISBN 0 540 08379 8
© Philip's 2003

This product includes mapping data licensed
from Ordnance Survey®, with the
permission of the Controller of Her Majesty's
Stationery Office.© Crown copyright 2003.
All rights reserved.
Licence number 100011710

The bus route maps on pages 80-82 are
reproduced with the permission of Lothian
Buses

Photographic acknowledgements:
vi bottom left, Dave Bartruff/CORBIS • vi top
right, Wild Country/CORBIS • vii bottom,
Derek Croucher/CORBIS

Printed and bound in Spain
by Cayfosa-Quebecor.

Contents

Key to map symbols

Roads

(12)	**Motorway** with junction number
A42	**Primary route** – dual/single carriageway
A42	**A road** – dual/single carriageway
B1289	**B road** – dual/single carriageway
	Through-route – dual/single carriageway
	Minor road – dual/single carriageway
	Rural track, private road or narrow road in urban area
	Path, bridleway, byway open to all traffic, road used as a public path
	Road under construction
	Pedestrianised area
	Gate or obstruction to traffic restrictions may not apply at all times or to all vehicles
P P&R	**Parking, Park and Ride**

Railways

	Railway
	Miniature railway
	Metro station, private railway station

Emergency services

	Ambulance station, coastguard station
	Fire station, police station
H +	**Hospital, Accident and Emergency entrance to hospital**

General features

+ PO	**Place of worship, Post Office**
i	**Information centre** (open all year)
	Bus, coach station
	Important buildings, schools, colleges, universities and hospitals
	Woods, built-up area
Tumulus FORT	**Non-Roman antiquity, Roman antiquity**

Leisure facilities

Δ 🚐	**Camping site, caravan site**
▶ ✕	**Golf course, picnic site**

Boundaries

••••••••	**Postcode boundaries**
—•—	**County and unitary authority boundaries**

Water features

River Ouse	**Tidal water, water name**
	Non-tidal water – lake, river, canal or stream
‹	**Lock, weir**

Scales

Blue pages: 4½ inches to 1 mile 1:14 080

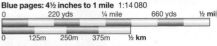

0   220 yds   ¼ mile   660 yds   ½ mi

0   125m   250m   375m   ½ km

Red pages: 7 inches to 1 mile 1:9051

0   110 yds   220 yds   330 yds   ¼ mile

0   125m   250m   375m   ½km

74   **Adjoining page indicators** The colour of the arrow and the band indicates the scale of the adjoining page (see above)

Abbreviations

Acad	Academy	Mkt	Market
Allot Gdns	Allotments	Meml	Memorial
Cemy	Cemetery	Mon	Monument
C Ctr	Civic Centre	Mus	Museum
CH	Club House	Obsy	Observatory
Coll	College	Pal	Royal Palace
Crem	Crematorium	PH	Public House
Ent	Enterprise	Recn Gd	Recreation Ground
Ex H	Exhibition Hall	Resr	Reservoir
Ind Est	Industrial Estate	Ret Pk	Retail Park
IRB Sta	Inshore Rescue Boat Station	Sch	School
		Sh Ctr	Shopping Centre
Inst	Institute	TH	Town Hall/House
Ct	Law Court	Trad Est	Trading Estate
L Ctr	Leisure Centre	Univ	University
LC	Level Crossing	Wks	Works
Liby	Library	YH	Youth Hostel

III

Key to map pages

63	Atlas pages at 7 inches to 1 mile
42	Atlas pages at 4½ inches to 1 mile

Scale

0   1   2   3   4   5   6 km
0   1   2   3 miles

Kinghorn

Burntisland

Inverkeithing

Cramond
2   3   4   5   Granton   6   7   8   9
West Pilton   Newhaven   Leith
Cramond Bridge   Davidson's Mains
Barnton   Drylaw   Bonnington   Hermitage
10   11   12   13   14   15   16   17   18   19
Edinburgh   Abbeyhill
West Craig   Murrayfield   62   64   Portobello
20   21   Joppa
Corstorphine   63   65   28   29
South Gyle   22   23   Fountainbridge   Dumbiedykes   Duddingston   Musselburgh
Saughton   Gorgie   24   25   26   27   Inveresk
32   33   34   35   The Grange   Craigmillar   30   31
Hermiston   Sighthill   Craiglockhart   36   37   38   39   Greendykes   Newcraighall
Wester Hailes   Morningside   West Mains   40   41   42   43
Riccarton   44   45   46   47   Greenbank   50   51   Danderhall   Millerhill
Juniper Green   Colinton   48   49   Gracemount   52   53   54   55
Fairmilehead   Kaimes   Gilmerton
Currie   Swanston   Muirhouse   60   61   Eskbank   Dalkeith
Balerno   56   57   58   59   Wadingburn
Hillend   Straiton
Loanhead
Newtongrange
Bonnyrigg and Lasswade
Roslin
Penicuik   Gorebridge

V

O F   F O R T H

Inchkeith

Route planning

Scale

0   1   2   3   4 km

Granton
Harbour

H.M.Y.
BRITANNIA

A901
Leith Docks
Newhaven

Leith

Trinity
ROAD   A902
Leith Links

Leith
Warriston
ROYAL
BOTANIC
GARDEN

New Town
Calton
Hill
MUS. OF
CHILDHOOD
LONDON   ROAD
Restalrig

Golf
Co.
Craigentinny

A199

A6140

Portobello

Joppa

MUSSELBURGH

Abbeyhill
CENTRAL
WAVERLEY
PALACE OF
HOLYROODHOUSE
GILES
CATHEDRAL
ROYAL
MILE
MUS. OF SCOTLAND
Univ
EDINBURGH 822
PLEASANCE
CASTLE
Old Town
Meadow
Park
Holyrood Pk.
Arthur's Seat

Duddingston

MILTON
A1
MILTON   RD.

MILTON RD. 2

A199 EAST
STA.

Newhailes

Fisherrow
MUSSELBURGH
LINKFIELD   RD.
Pinkie H.

Newington
BRUNTSFIELD
Duddingston L.
Golf Co.
Prestonfield
Golf Co.
Bingham
Southfield
Craigmillar

RD. WEST

A6095

Inveresk
Stoneybank
INVERESK
LODGE
GARDENS
Newcraighall
STA.
Golf Co.
Monktonhall

1547

Morningside
OBSERVATORY
Blackford
Hill
Univ.
Golf Co.
Nether Liberton
Bridge End
A6095
CRAIGMILLAR
CASTLE
Niddrie

Cauldcoats

Old
Craighall
Whitecraig
EDINBURGH
SERVICES
A1
Carberry

Braid
Liberton
Dams
Liberton Tr.
GILMERTON   ROAD
Golf
Co.
Edmonstone
Hilltown

A6124

OLD   CRAIGHALL

Smeaton

Braid Hills
Golf Courses
Mortonhall
Moredun
Danderhall
Harelaw
Millerhill

Carbe
Tow

Smeaton
Shaw

Fairmilehead
Kaimes
Liberton
A7
Drum
Mains
Sheriffhall
Mains
THE   CITY   OF   EDINBURGH   BY-PASS
River
ESK
SALTER'S ROAD
A6094
B6414
Carbe

Burdiehouse
B701
BY-PASS
West Edge
A720
Gilmerton
Campend
A768
Dalkeith Ho.
DALKEITH PARK
Dalkeith
A68
W. Cowden

Lothianburn
Damhead
Holdings
Straiton
Melville
Mains
EDINBURGH BUTTERFLY
AND INSECT WORLD
Eskbank
Newbattle
Golf Co.
Whitehill

A702
A701
B7003
Edgefield
Nazareth
Ho.
Golf Co.
A7
Hardengreen
Easthouses
Lawfield

Loanhead
Old
Pentland
New Saughton
Hall
**Bonnyrigg and
Lasswade**
Polton
B704
Lothianbridge
Millhill Ho.
B6482
Mayfiel

Seafield
Bilston
Midfield Ho.
Poltonhall
Burnbrae
Newtongrange
D'Arcy
Ho.

Easter
Bush
Dryden

Sights of Edinburgh

One star * indicates highly recommended sights.

Two stars ** indicate sights of exceptional interest.

Historic buildings

Assembly Rooms * *54 George Street* Constructed in the 18th century for grand society gatherings; now a venue for cultural events. Scott, Thackeray and Dickens all appeared here in their day. ℂ0131 220 4349 *62 C4*

City Observatory *Calton Hill* This walled complex includes the domed City Observatory, designed by William Playfair with the two-faced 'Politician's Clock'; the Old Observatory House, a rare surviving work by New Town planner James Craig; and Playfair's Doric Monument. Visits by arrangement with the Astronomical Society. ℂ0131 667 0647 *64 B4*

Craigmillar Castle *Craigmillar* A magnificent ruin complete with battlements and curtain walls, best known for having put up Mary, Queen of Scots for a few nights. ℂ0131 661 4445 *39 C2*

Edinburgh Castle ** *Castlehill* Scotland's most visited attraction includes tiny St Margaret's Chapel (Edinburgh's oldest church), the Honours of Scotland (crown jewels), the Scottish National War Memorial, four military museums, the apartments of Mary, Queen of Scots, the One O'Clock Gun, and Mons Meg cannon. ℂ0131 668 8800 *62 C3*

Gladstone's Land * *477b Lawnmarket* This city's best sur-

▼ *John Knox's House*

viving 17th-century tenement (apartment block), restored by the National Trust for Scotland. ℂ0131 226 5856 *64 A3*

Greyfriars Kirk *Candlemaker Row* The city's first post-Reformation church, best known as the place where the National Covenant was signed in 1638. Its graveyard contains many famous names, including Greyfriars Bobby, the Skye terrier said to have mourned his master here for 14 years. ℂ0131 225 1900 *65 A2*

Palace of Holyroodhouse and Holyrood Abbey ** *Holyrood Road* The Queen's official Scottish residence includes Queen Victoria's dining room, the bedroom of Charles II, and the state apartments of Mary, Queen of Scots. The new Queen's Gallery is an offshoot of the Royal Collection in London. The ruined abbey was founded by David I in 1128. ℂ0131 556 1096 *64 C3*

St Cecilia's Hall *Niddry Street* Scotland's first purpose-built concert hall (mid 18th century), restored in the 1950s. As well as hosting concerts, it is home to the world-class Russell Collection of Early Keyboard Instruments. ℂ0131 650 2805 *64 B3*

Houses

Georgian House * *7 Charlotte Square* A re-creation of a Georgian residence by the National Trust for Scotland. ℂ0131 226 3318 *62 B3*

Goose Pie House *Ramsay Garden* An octagonal house built by 18th-century poet Allan Ramsay and altered in the late 19th century by Patrick Geddes, preserver of much of the Royal Mile. Only the exterior is viewable. *62 C3*

John Knox's House *43 High Street* A 16th-century house restored by virtue of its association with the fiery preacher, who is said to have died (though not necessarily lived) here. ℂ0131 556 9579 *64 B3*

Green spaces

Hermitage of Braid * *Braid Hills* A wooded dell with nature trails, a burn, a teashop and education centre in an 18th-century house. *37 B1*

▲ *National Gallery, Edinburgh*

Holyrood Park ** *Queen's Drive* Home to the extinct volcano of Arthur's Seat, this royal park is home to various rare forms of wildlife and ancient geological features. ℂ *27 A3*

The Meadows *Southside* The site of the city's 19th-century Great Exhibition, these green expanses were once used by the city's professional football teams. ℂ *65 A1*

Royal Botanic Garden ** *Arboretum Place and Inverleith Row* The 'Botanics' was founded as a Physic Garden for the Palace of Holyroodhouse in 1670; the glasshouses, Fossil Garden and Chinese Collection are highlights, and Inverleith House hosts modern art exhibitions. ℂ0131 552 7171 *15 A3*

Places of worship

High Kirk of St Giles *High Street (at Parliament Square)* Edinburgh's first parish church, though the tower is medieval and most of the exterior was designed by William Burn in the early 1800s. During the Reformation, John Knox preached here. ℂ0131 225 4363 *64 A3*

Museums and galleries

Dean Gallery ** *73 Belford Road* Housed in the former Dean Orphanage, this is home to the Gallery of Modern Art's collection of Surrealist and Dada works. ℂ0131 624 6200 *24 B4*

Talbot Rice Gallery * *Old College, South Bridge* Housed in the Robert Adam-designed Old College, this gallery hosts the University's art collection and exhibitions of contemporary art. ℂ0131 650 2211 *65 A2*

Museum of Childhood *42 High Street* Displays of toys going

back several generations, with an activity area and children's library. ℂ0131 529 4142 *64 B3*

Museum of Edinburgh *Huntly House, 142 Canongate* The largest local history museum, set in three 16th-century townhouses. ℂ0131 529 4143 *64 B3*

Museum of Scotland ** *Chambers Street* A world-class museum in a modern building inspired by a range of historic native architecture, tracing the story of Scottish life from prehistory to the present. ℂ0131 247 4027 *65 A2*

National Gallery of Scotland * *The Mound* A splendid art collection housed in a William Playfair-designed Greek temple, it incorporates the longterm loan of the Duke of Sutherland's exceptional private collection. ℂ0131 624 6200 *62 C3*

Newhaven Heritage Museum * *24 Pier Place, Newhaven* A small local history museum dedicated to life in this former fishing village. ℂ0131 551 4165 *7 C3*

Royal College of Surgeons *9 Hill Square* Set in an Ionic temple designed by William Playfair in the early 19th century, this comprises an exhibition about the history of surgery, a dental museum, and a pathology museum. ℂ0131 527 1600 *65 B2*

Royal Museum ** *Chambers Street* Britain's largest all-encompassing museum, roughly divided into the Natural World and the Decorative Arts. The 'Connected Earth' gallery (opening in autumn 2003) covers the history of telecommunications, with a special focus on Alexander Graham Bell. ℂ0131 247 4027 *65 A2*

Royal Scottish Academy *The Mound* The RSA hosts bi-annual shows by its members and

other annual exhibitions. A massive renovation of this William Playfair-designed Greek temple is scheduled for completion in August 2003. ☎0131 225 6671 62 C3

Scottish National Gallery of Modern Art ★★ *75 Belford Road* Britain's first national gallery devoted to modern art, housed in a neo-classical building dating from 1825. Works are hung on rotation; strengths include early 20th-century French art. There is also a sculpture garden. ☎0131 624 6200 24 A4

Scottish National Portrait Gallery *1 Queen Street* Most of Scotland's greats can be found at the NPG, gifted to the city by *Scotsman* proprietor Ritchie Findlay in 1882. ☎0131 624 6200 64 A4

Writers' Museum ★ *Makar's Close* A restored 17th-century house that now commemorates the lives and works of Robert Burns, Sir Walter Scott and Robert Louis Stevenson. ☎0131 529 4901 64 A3

Activities

Edinburgh Festival ★★
Throughout the city This world-famous performing arts festival (actually five festivals: the International Festival; the comedy-dominated Fringe; the Military Tattoo; the International Book Festival; the International Film Festival; and the industry Television Festival) takes over the city, from its theatres to its open spaces and underground vaults, throughout August. ☎0131 473 2000 (Int)/226 5257 (Fringe)/225 1188 (Tattoo)/228 5444 (Book)/221 8715 (Film)/(020) 7430 1333 (TV)

Golf Links *Various* Edinburgh may have been home to the world's first golf club and has a number of 'links' (technically, seaside courses). The tourist board sells a discount golf pass to 20 Lothians courses (four in the city). ☎0131 473 3800

Hogmanay ★★ *Throughout the city* Edinburgh's famously exuberant New Year celebrations; free tickets for the Royal Bank Street party must be booked well in advance. ☎0131 473 2000

Jenners *48 Princes Street* The world's oldest department store, set up in 1895 and known as the 'Harrods of Scotland'. ☎0131 225 2442 64 A3

Leith Waterworld *377 Easter Road* A state-of-the-art waterpark complete with swimming pool, wave machines, flumes and the like. ☎0131 555 6000 16 C4

Our Dynamic Earth ★ *Holyrood Road* A child-oriented geological attraction with an earthquake simulator, a mockup rainforest and hi-tech audiovisual displays. ☎0131 550 7800 64 C3

Water of Leith ★ *Across the city* Edinburgh's former industrial waterway now forms a tranquil walkway though the city. The Visitor Centre on Lanark Road has displays on history and wildlife. ☎0131 455 7367 23 B2

Other sights

Britannia, Former Royal Yacht ★ *Ocean Terminal, Leith* Decommissioned in 1997, *Britannia* gives an insight into the lives of the royal family. ☎0131 555 5566 8 B3

Caledonian Brewery *42 Slateford Road* A still-functioning 19th-century brewery, of which tasting tours are available. ☎0131 337 1286 24 A1

Camera Obscura and World of Illusions *549 Castlehill* Two 17th-century tenements transformed into an observatory by optician Maria Short in 1852. The original Camera Obscura is still there; other rooms have holograms and similar visual tricks. ☎0131 226 3709 62 C3

Dean Cemetery ★ *Dean Path* A crowded, atmospheric graveyard containing flamboyant mausolea and monuments to some famous citizens. 14 B1

Discovery Room *52 Queen Street* A museum of the introduction of anaesthesia, pioneered by Sir James Young Simpson, who lived in this early New Town house. ☎0131 225 6028 64 C4

Edinburgh Old Town Weaving Company *555 Castlehill* Learn about the history of tartan and to see it being made. ☎0131 226 1555 62 C3

Edinburgh Zoo *Corstorphine Road* Affording fine views from Corstorphine Hill, Edinburgh Zoo includes an otter enclosure and daily penguin-feeding sessions in summer (2pm). ☎0131 334 9171 22 B3

Mary King's Close ★ *Beneath City Chambers, High Street* One of the city's eerie 'buried streets', with the vaults where plague victims were sealed up alive, accessible by guided tour. ☎0131 557 6464 (Mercat Tours) 64 A3

Moray Place ★ *New Town* A well-preserved Roman-Doric-style circus, the centrepiece of the third and most successful New Town development. ☎ 62 B4

National Monument *Calton Hill* Intended as a memorial to the Napoleonic Wars dead, but funds ran dry and it was dubbed 'Edinburgh's folly'. A popular viewpoint. ☎ 64 B4

Royal Mile ★★ *Edinburgh's main street* (known variously as Castlehill, Lawnmarket, High Street and Canongate) Tracing a more or less straight line from the Castle to the Palace of Holyroodhouse, the Royal Mile is bordered by historic 'lands' (tenements) and 'closes' (tiny cobbled alleys) and takes in some of the city's major attractions. ☎ 62 C3, 64 A3, 64 B3

Scotch Whisky Heritage Centre *354 Castlehill* An exhibition on the history of the water of life. ☎0131 220 0441 62 C3

Scott Monument ★ *East Princes Street Gardens* A landmark Gothic monument with a huge statue of Sir Walter and 64 statuettes of figures from Scottish history and characters from his novels. The top gallery has panoramic sea and city views. ☎0131 529 4068 63 A3

Information

Scotrail ☎08457 484950
Traveline Scotland ☎0870 608 2608
Lothian Buses *27 Hanover Street and Waverley Bridge (Travelshops)* ☎0131 555 6363
Car Parking City Council ☎0131 469 5400
Car Parking NCP ☎0131 229 2870
Edinburgh Airport ☎0131 333 1000
Tourist Information *3 Princes Street* ☎0131 473 3800 64 A3 *and Edinburgh Airport*

Edinburgh Castle

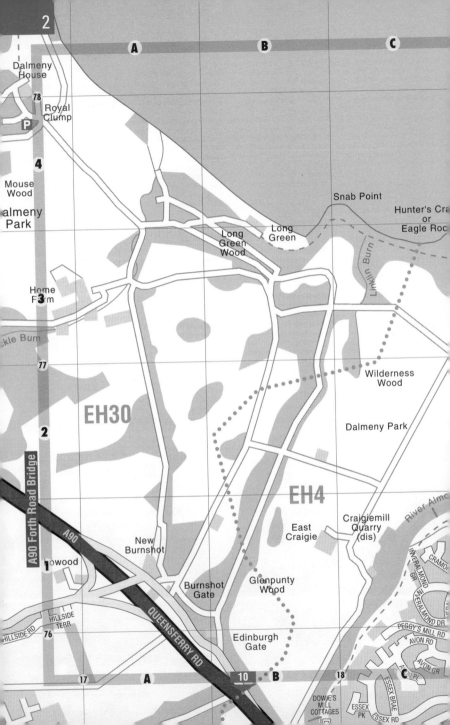

The Knoll

A   B   C

78

4

Firth of Forth

The Binks

785

Cramond Island

The Knoll

3

Breakwater

4

195

1 CRAMOND VILLAGE
2 RIVERSIDE

77

Cobble
Cottage

P

Tower

MARINE DR

P

Ferry

CRAMOND GLEBE RD

CRAMOND
ROMAND FORT

OND GLEBE TERR 1
THE GLEBE 2
OND BANK COTTS 3
ELL'S ROW COTTS 4
AIR-A-FAR COTTS 5

Cramond House

KIRK CRAMOND

2

CRAMOND GLEBE GDNS

1
2

PO

SCHOOL BRAE

3 Sch
(Annexe)

CRAMOND GN

CRAMOND GLEBE

Moray House
Coll of Ed

4

5

CRAMOND TERR

CRAMOND PL

CRAMOND AVE

CRAMOND PK

CRAMOND GR

CRAMOND GDNS

CRAMOND RD N

1

FAR

Sch

CRAMOND CRES

CRAMOND BANK

GAMEKEEPER'S
LOAN

Double Dykes

S

Laur
Cas

GAMEKEEPER'S
R-A-FAR
PK

GAMEKEEPER'S RD

KING'S CRAMOND

Cramond

EH4

CRAMOND RD S

76

BARNTON GDNS

COTTAGE
GN
OND REGIS

Cargilfield
Sch

Quarry
(disused)

NORTHLAWN
TERR

EASTER PARK DR

F

BARNTON
BRAE

BARNTON AVE W

CT

A   19   B   11   C   20   CH

BARNT

78

4

3

3

77

2

Firth of Forth

MARINE DR

MARINE DR

Hotel

MARINE

P

SILVERKNOWES RD

EH4

Silverknowes

1

Lauriston
Castle

CH

SILVERKNOWES PARKWAY

MUIRHOUS

MUIRHOUSE
VIEW

PO

MUIRHOUSE GR

MUIRHOUSE GDNS

Sch

CRAIGROYSTON
PL

MEDWAY

76

Quarry
(disused)

CH

CRAMOND RD S

BARNTON GDNS

NORTHLAWN
TERR

EASTER PARK DR

P

SILVERKNOWE
LOAN

20

A

LAURISTON FARM RD

SILVERKNOWES
CRES

12

SILVERKNOWES
HILL

SILVERKNOWES
PL

SILVERKNOWES
GR

SILVERKNOWES
RD

B

SILVERKNOWES GDNS

SILVERKNOWES
CT

SILVERKNOWES
BANK

SILVERKNOWES
EASTWAY

SILVERKNOWES DR

21

CRAIGROYSTON
GR

MUIRHOUSE PK

MUIRHOUSE
GN

CL

C

MUIF

MUI

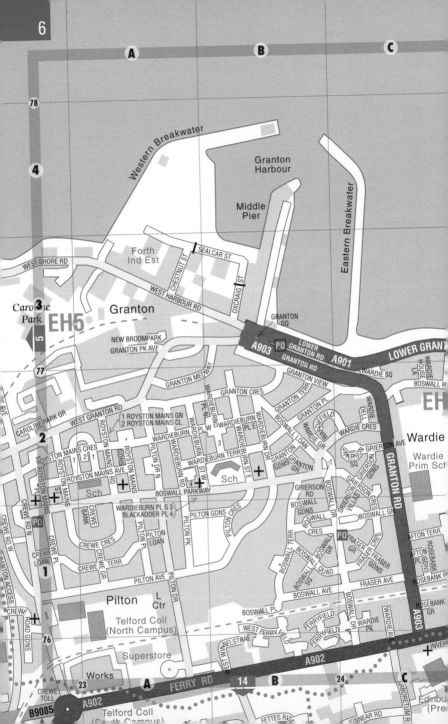

A B C

78

4

Firth of Forth

West Breakwater

Sports Ctr

Western Harbour

Hotel

ANDREW WOOD CT 5
WESTMOST CL 6
LAMBS CT 7
WESTER CL 8
FISHMARKET SQ 9
GREAT MICHAEL SQ 10
GREAT MICHAEL CL 11
PEACOCK CT 12

Newhaven Heritage Mus

LAVEROCKBANK AVE 1
LAVEROCK BANK GDNS 2
MAYVILLE GDNS 3
MAYVILLE GDNS E 4

Newhaven Harbour

3

Mills

PIER PL A901

77

TRINITY CRES STARBANK RD

NEWHAVEN MAIN ST

LINDSAY RD

NORTH LE

PRIMROSE BANK RD

LAVEROCKBANK CRES

WILLOWBANK ROW
AUCHINLECK CT

Sch

MICH

ANNFIELD ST

BATHFIELD

NORTH
FIELD

PARK RD

PARK PL

JESSFIELD
TERR

HAWTHORNVALE

NICHOLLFIELD

HILLH

LENNOX ROW

LAVEROCKBANK
TERR

SOUTH
LAVEROCKBANK
AVE

PARK PL
SOUTH
PK

DERBY ST

PO Newhaven

DUDLEY BANK

NORTH LE

FORT
HO

STIRLING
RD

YORK
RD

RUSSEL PL

LAVEROCKBANK
GR

ROSEVILLE
GDNS

BELVEDERE

3 4

STANLEY RD
WEST
RRYBANK

DUDLEY CRES

DUDLEY
TERR

DUDLEY
GR

HAWTHORNBANK

NEW
HAWTHORN PL

DUDLEY AVE

FORT

LAPICIDE
PL

LAND PL

CAITHNESS
PL

TRINITY

SPENCER
PL

TRINITY GR

TRINITY
MAINS

LIXMOUNT
GDNS

CRAIGHALL
CRES

CRAIGHALL
AVE

Trinity
Acad

DUDLEY GDNS

SUMMERSIDE ST

INDUSTRY
LA

MADEIR

IL TERR

EARL HAIG
GDNS

LILLYPOT

EAST TRINITY RD

BERESFORD
AVE

GRANDVILLE

CRAIGHALL
BANK

Trinity
Pnm Sch

EH6

SUMMERSIDE PL

Sch

DENHAM
GREEN PL

TRINITY WAY

EAST
BANGHOLM

BERESFORD
GDNS

GRANDFIELD

NEWHAVEN RD

RD

DENHAM
GREEN TERR

CLARK RD

LILLYPOT

BANGHOLM
BOWER

CRAIGHALL GDNS

A902

PO

SOUTH FOR

ROSE
PK

SOUTH TRINITY RD

CLARK
RD

BANGHOLM
BOWER AVE

BANGHOLM
RD

BANGHOLM VIEW

CRAIGHALL TERR

NEW CUT RIGG

BONNINGTON
TERR

TRAFALGAR
ST

1

PITT ST

WEST BOWLING

HILL TERR

BANGHOLM
LOAN

BANGHOLM
AVE

Sch

CHANCELOT
TERR

MULBERRY
PL

GRAHAM ST

FERRY RD

CHANCELOT
CRES

BONAR PL

AGNEW
PL

GOSFORD PL

BONNINGTON
AVE

KINGHORN
PL

BONNINGTON

Bonnington Mill
Bs s Ctr

B90

MONMOUTH TERR

ROYSTON TERR

PO

GOLDENACRE TERR

EASTER WARRISTON

CHANCELOT
GR

DALMENY RD

CONNAUGHT PL

WHITINGFORD

MILN-ACRE

BONNYHAUGH

BLEACHFIELD

ELIZAFIELD

Bonnington
Ind Est

RONDA

INVERLEITH AVE

BANGHOLM
TERR

Goldenacre

25

WARRISTON GDNS

WARRISTON RD

Crem

LADEHEAD

BONNYHAUGH
LA

STEWARTFIELD

ASHLEY PL

PO

B 15

Cemy

C Bonnington 26

Pi
Ind

Warriston

Water of Leith

REDBRAES
GR

REDBRAES PL

GIBSON ST

Pip

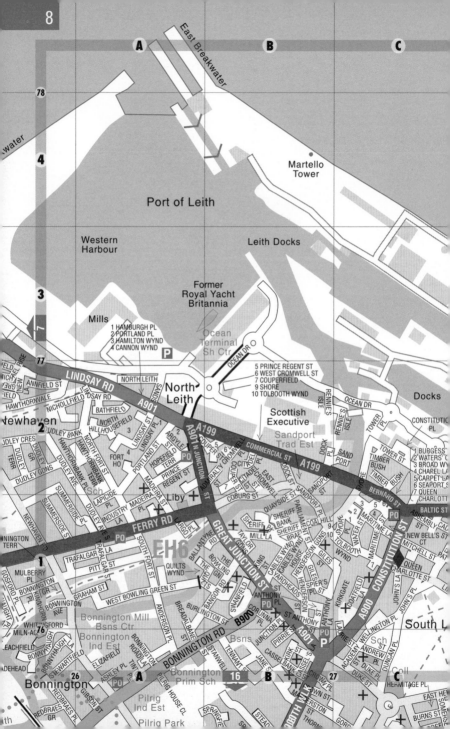

East Breakwater

A   B   C

78

4

Martello
Tower

Port of Leith

Western
Harbour

Leith Docks

3

Former
Royal Yacht
Britannia

Mills

1 HAMBURGH PL
2 PORTLAND PL
3 HAMILTON WYND
4 CANNON WYND

Ocean
Terminal
Sh Ctr

77

LINDSAY RD   A901

NORTH LEITH

North
Leith

5 PRINCE REGENT ST
6 WEST CROMWELL ST
7 COUPERFIELD
9 SHORE
10 TOLBOOTH WYND

OCEAN DR

Docks

Scottish
Executive

RENNIE'S ISLE

OCEAN DR

TOWER

CONSTITUTION
PL

Newhaven

ANNFIELD ST

NICHOLLFIELD

LINDSAY RD

HAWTHORNVALE

BATHFIELD

NORTH
HILLHOUSEFIELD

A901 JUNCTION

A199

COMMERCIAL ST   A199

Sandport
Trad Est

DOCK
PL

SAND
PORT

TIMBER
BUSH

TOWER ST

TIMBER
BUSH

1 BURGESS
2 WATER'S
3 BROAD W
4 CHAREL LA
5 CARPET LA
6 SEAPORT
7 QUEEN
CHARLOTT

2

DUDLEY BANK

DUDLEY CRES

DUDLEY
GR

DUDLEY
TERR

DUDLEY GDNS

DUDLEY AVE

SUMMERSIDE PL

NEWHAVEN RD

FANTTHORNBANK PL

HAWTHORNBANK

NORTH FORT ST

FORT
HO

LINDSAY ST

LINDSAY PL

PORTLAND ST

ARGYLE

HOPEFIELD
TERR

PRINCE
REGENT ST

Sch

LAPICIDE
PL

MADEIRA ST

MADEIRA
PL

INDUSTRY
LA

COUPER ST

ADMIRALTY ST

CITADEL

CROMWELL
ST

EAST
CROMWELL ST

COBURG ST

CITADEL ST

SANDPORT PL

QUAYSIDE ST

DOCK ST

SHERIFF
BANK

SHERIFF
BRAE

COALHILL

SHORE

BERNARD ST

BALTIC ST

PO

ASSEMBLY

NEW BELL'S
CT

MITCHELL ST

QUEEN
CHARLOTTE ST

Liby

FERRY RD

CARGO PL

GREAT JUNCTION ST

A901 JUNCTION

SHERIFF
MILL LA

PARLIAMENT ST

KING ST

CABLES WYND

MARITIME ST

MARITIME LA

1

MULBERRY
PL

BONNINGTON

KINGHORN

BONNINGTON
AVE

GRAHAM ST

PITT ST

TRAFALGAR ST

TRAFALGAR LA

SOUTH FORT ST

QUILTS
WYND

WEST BOWLING GREEN ST

BOWLING
GREEN ST

BALLANTYNE PL

THE
GR

BANGOR
RD

SWANFIELD

BREADALBANE ST

CORUNNA
PL

ST
ANTHONY
PL

ST ANTHONY
LA

HENDERSON
HOUSE

CABLES WYND

YARDHEADS

GILES ST

SPIER'S
PL

GILES ST

HENDERSON
GDNS

TOLBOOTH
WYND

WATER ST

KIRKGATE

LAURIE ST

COATFIELD

JOHN'S PL

WELLINGTON PL

DUNCAN PL

CONSTITUTION ST   A900

CHARLOTTE ST

John's La

South L

EH6

GOSFORD PL

WHITTINGFORD

MILN-AC

BEACHFIELD

DEHEAD

NEWINGTON
TERR

BONNINGTON RD   B900

Bonnington Mill
Bsns Ctr

Bonnington
Ind Est

BONNINGTON
ROAD LA

ANDERSON PL

BURLINGTON ST

Bsns

STANWELL
ST

TENNANT
ST

JANE ST

PIRRIE ST

CASSELBANK ST

CASSEL
ST

KIRK ST

ST ANTHONY

CROWN ST

A901

PO

ACADEMY ST

ANDREW ST

DUKE ST

Sch

DUNCAN PL

Coll

HERMITAGE PL

EAST HE

Bonnington

26

BONNYHAUGH

STEWARTFIELD

ASHLEY PL

PILRIG HOUSE CL

ELIZAFIELD

GIBSON ST

Bonnington
Prim Sch

16

PILRIG ST

SPRINGFIE

27

DUKE ST

BURNS SO

REDBRAES
GR

Pilrig
Ind Est

Pilrig Park

B

A **B** **C**

78

4

Works

Port of Leith

Firth of Forth

3

77

East Sands
of Leith

2

Leith

LC

BATH RD

ALBERT RD

EH6

SALAMANDER ST

CARRON PL

MARINE ESPL

1

LINKS GARDENS LA
LINKS GDNS

ST
SALAMANDER PL
LINKS GDNS

76

Sewage
Works

St Mary's (Leith)
RC Prim Sch

SALAMANDER YDS

SEAFIELD
PL

eith
nks

LINKS GDNS

GLAD STONE
PL

SUMMERFIELD
GDNS

CLAREMONT PK

A 28

BOO

B 17

LC **C** 29

SEAFIELD RD

Seafield

PO

IAL RD

SUMMERFIELD
PL

BLACKIE RD

REMONT RD

CLAREMONT GDNS

PIRNIEFIELD
TERR

PROSPECT

CRE LA PIRNIEFI

FIELD PL

ABEELD ST

Cemy

Crem

**Claremont
Park**

STALRIG

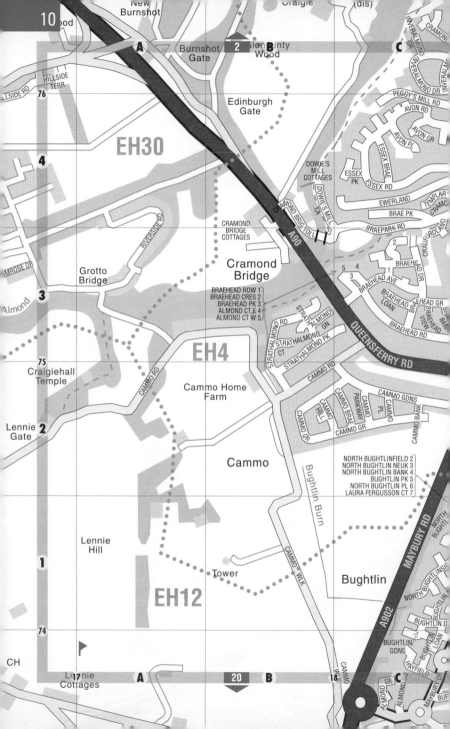

New Burnshot

Craigie (dis)

Burnshot Gate
A
2
Glen Bunty Wood
B
C

HILLSIDE TERR
76
LLSIDE RD

Edinburgh Gate

INVERALMOND
CRAMON
INVERALMOND DR
NVERALMOND
INVERALMOND

PEGGY'S MILL RD

AVON RD
AVON GR
AVON PL

EH30

DOWIE'S MILL COTTAGES

ESSEX PK
ESSEX BRAE
ESSEX RD
EWERLAND
TEMPLAR
CRAMO

4

MBROSE DR

Grotto Bridge

RIVERSIDE RD

CRAMOND BRIDGE COTTAGES

DOWIE'S MILL
LA
CRAMOND BRIG TOLL
A90

BRAE PK
CRAUFURDLAND

BRAEPARK RD

Cramond Bridge

Almond

3

BRAEHEAD ROW 1
BRAEHEAD CRES 2
BRAEHEAD PK 3
ALMOND CT E 4
ALMOND CT W 5

2
5 4 1
3
BRAEHEAD AVE
BRAEHEAD DR
BRAEHEAD GR
BRAEHEAD BANK
BRAEHEAD LOAN
BRAEHEAD VIEW
QUEENSFERRY RD

STRATHALMOND RD
STRATH ALMOND CT
ALMOND GN

EH4

75

Craigiehall Temple

CAMMO RD

Cammo Home Farm

STRATHALMOND PK
STRATHALMOND RD
CAMMO RD

CAMMO PARKWAY
CAMMO PL
CAMMO GDNS
CAMMO BANK

Lennie **2** Gate

CAMMO HILL
CAMMO BRAE
CAMMO GR
CAMMO GR

Cammo

Bughtlin Burn

NORTH BUGHTLINFIELD 2
NORTH BUGHTLIN NEUK 3
NORTH BUGHTLIN BANK 4
BUGHTLIN PK 5
NORTH BUGHTLIN PL 6
LAURA FERGUSSON CT 7

NORTH BUGHTLINSID
NORTH BUGHTLI

Lennie Hill

MAYBURY RD

BUGHTLIN D.
BUGHTLINSID

1

EH12

Tower

CAMMO WLK

Bughtlin

A902

BUGHTLIN LOAN
BUGHTLIN GDNS
HAYFIELD

74

CH

Lennie Cottages
A
20
B
18
CAMMO W
C

ALMOND GN
ALMOND Cd
MAYBURY RD
BUF

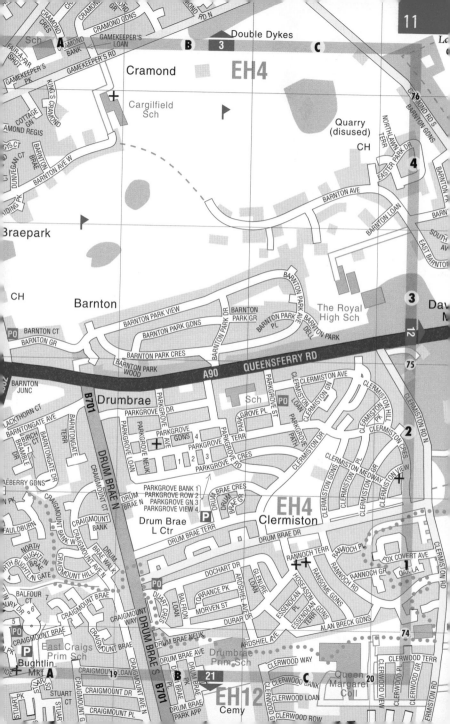

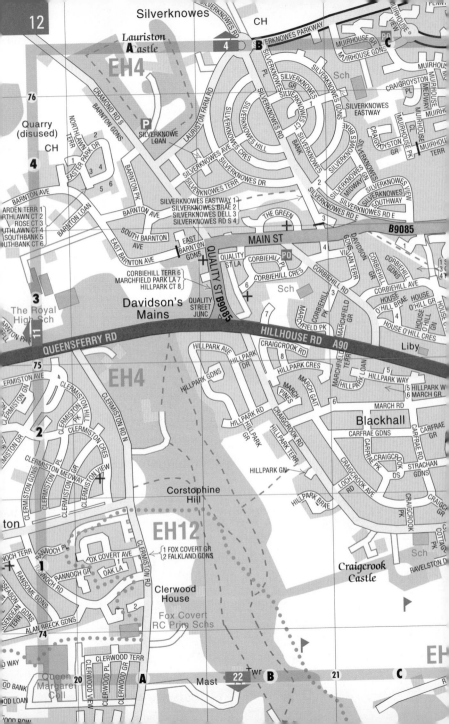

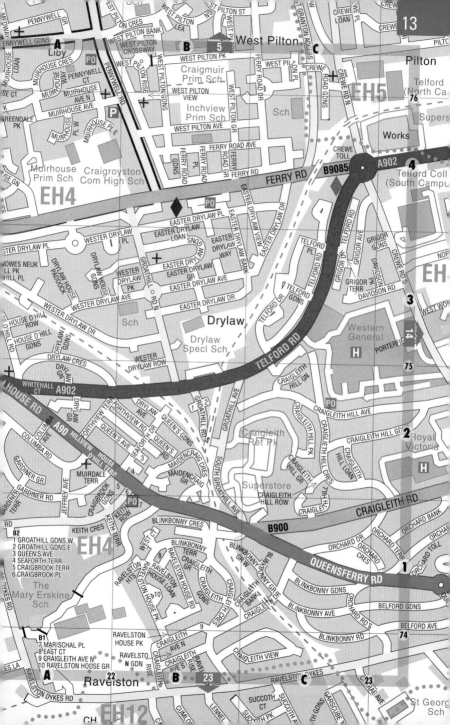

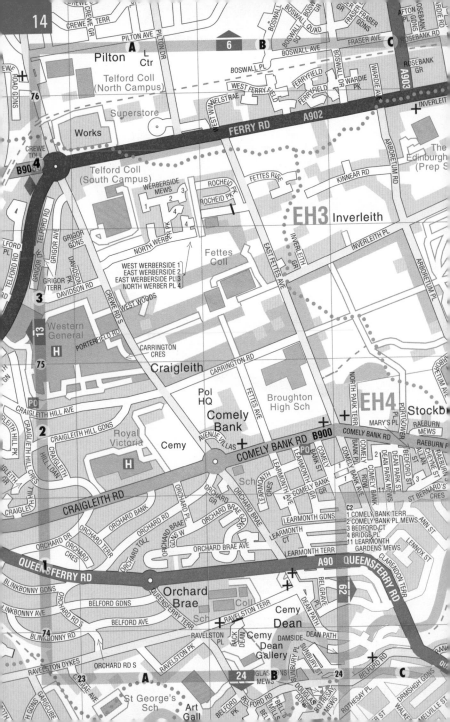

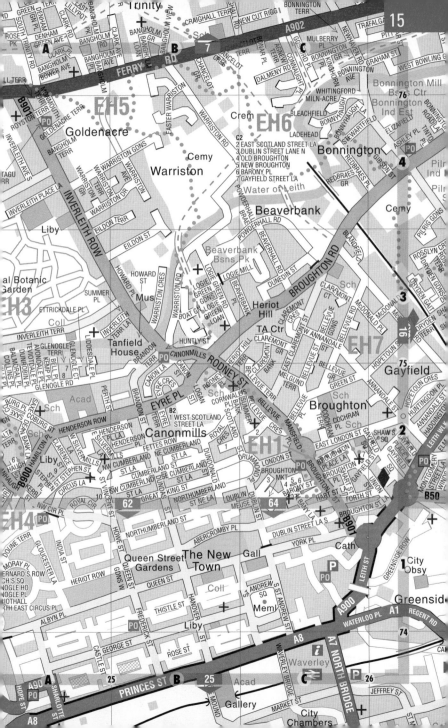

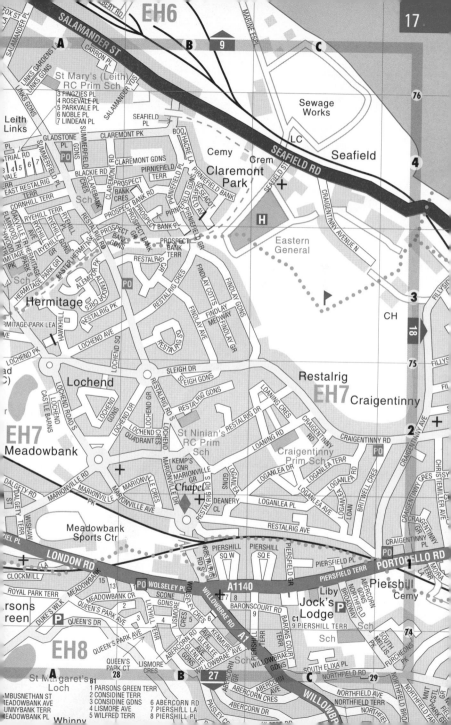

A   **B**   **C**

Firth of Forth

76
age rks

Seafield
4

CRAIGENTINNY AVENUE N

EH6

3

17

CH

75

estalrig

EH7 Craigentinny

FILLYSIDE RD

FILLYSIDE TERR

NANTWICH DR

SEAFIELD WAY

SEAFIELD ROAD E

PROMENADE

PO

FILLYSIDE AVE

Ind Est

EH15

STAPELEY AVE

1 ELECTRA PL
2 HILLCOAT LOAN
3 WESTBANK PL
4 WESTBANK LOAN
5 HILLCOAT PL
6 GREAT CANNON BANK

2

CRAIGENTINNY RD

PO

CRAIGENTINNY AVE

CRAIGENTINNY CRES

BRITWELL CRES

KEKEWICH AVE

WAKEFIELD AVE

BRYCE AVE

GOFF AVE

PROMENADE

HARBOUR PL 1
WILLIAM JAMESON PL 2
BRICKFIELD 3
LAW PL 4
THE POTTERY 5
SHRUB MOUNT 7
AITCHISON'S PL 8
WHINS PL 9

ntinny
Sch

LOGANLEA TERR

LOGANLEA RD

SYDNEY PL

SYDNEY TERR

SYDNEY

CHRISTIEMILLER AVE

CHRISTIEMILLER PL

VANDELEUR AVE

VANDELEUR

BRYCE GR

VANDELEUR GR

KING'S TERR

KING'S RD

AIGENTINNY RD

ANLEA AVE

LOGANLEA LOAN

CRAIGENTINNY GR

CRAIGENTINNY PL

CHRISTIEMILLER GR

INCHVIEW TERR   A1140

6
5
4
3
2
1

WESTBANK ST

L Ctr
P

HARBOUR

1 PIERSFIELD PL

PIERSFIELD TERR

PO

PORTOBELLO RD

MOIRA TERR

MOIRA

PARKER AVE

PARKER TERR

WEST TELFERTON

TELFERTON

EAST TELFERTON

SIR HARRY LAUDER RD

BAILEYFIELD RD

A199

PORTOBELLO HIGH ST

B6415

BRIDGE S
PIPE ST

Liby

Jock's Lodge

Piershill Cerny

1 MOUNTCASTLE GN
2 MOUNTCASTLE PL
3 MOUNTCASTLE PK

ABERCORN GDNS

ABERCORN BROADWAY

PARKER

FARRER

FARRER GR

FISHWIVES' CSWY

FISHWIVES' CSWY

BAILEYFIELD CRES

ADELPHI

ROSEFIELD AVE

ROSEFIELD PL

ROSEFIELD LA

Liby

74

Sch

Sch

SOUTH ELIXA PL

SOUTH MELLS

FURCHEONS PK

MOUNTCASTLE CRES

MOUNTCASTLE GDNS

MOUNTCASTLE TERR

Baileyfield Est

WEST BRIGHTON CRES

BRIGHTON PL

ROSEFIELD

EH8

NORTHFIELD RD

29

WILLOWB

NORTHFIELD AVE
NORTHFIELD TERR

MNT CSTL PK GR

NORTHFIELD BRO

MOUNTCASTLE PK

28   **B**

30   **C**

A6106

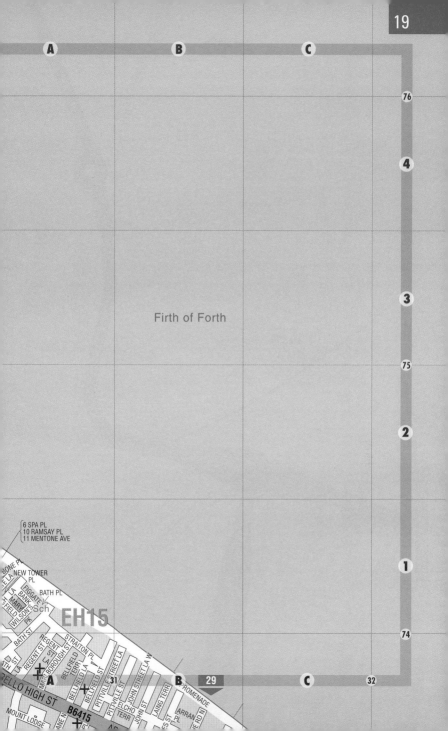

A

B

C

76

4

3

75

2

Firth of Forth

6 SPA PL
10 RAMSAY PL
11 MENTONE AVE

1

BONE PL
NEW TOWER
PL
LA
BANK
BATH PL
BIGGATE
FIELD
MARY
WILSON'S Sch
PK

EH15

74

BATH ST
REGENT
ST
STRAITON PL
REGENT
ST
BELLFIELD
TERR
MARLBOROUGH ST
ATH LA
BATH ST
BELLFIELD ST
BELLFIELD LA
PITVILLE ST
JOHN STREET LA
JOHN STREET LA W
ELCHO
TERR
LAING TERR
ARRAN
PL
E RD N
JOHN ST
SS ST

A

31

B

29

PROMENADE

C

32

LLO HIGH ST

B6415

MOUNT LODGE

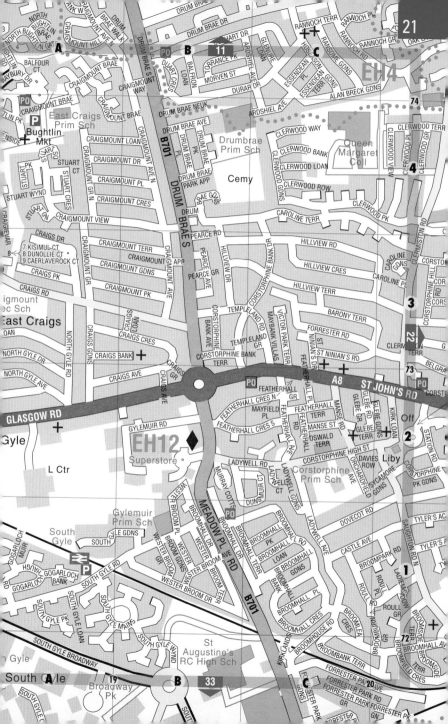

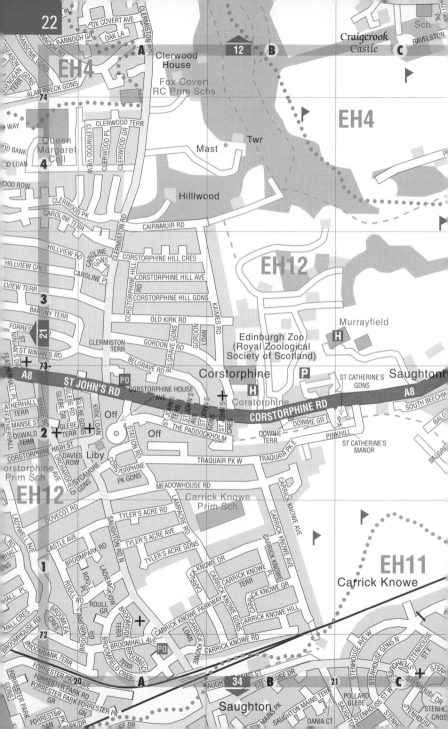

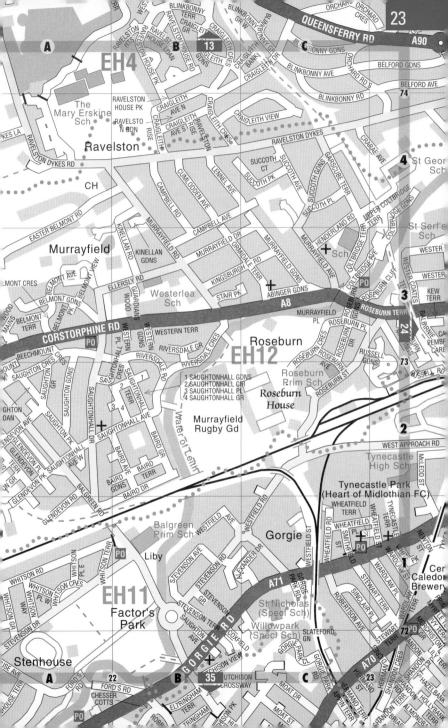

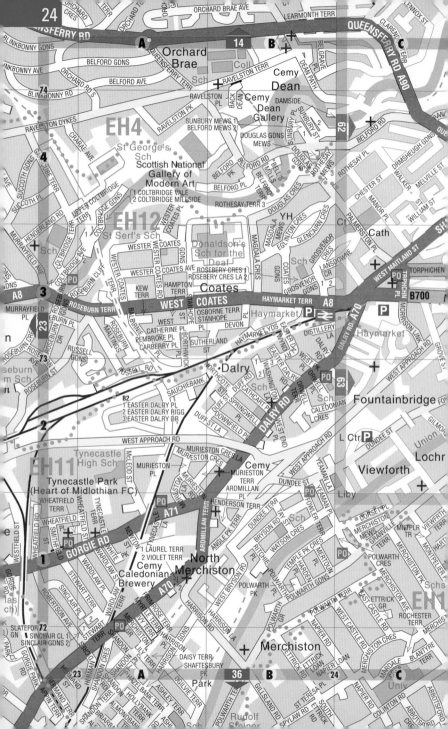

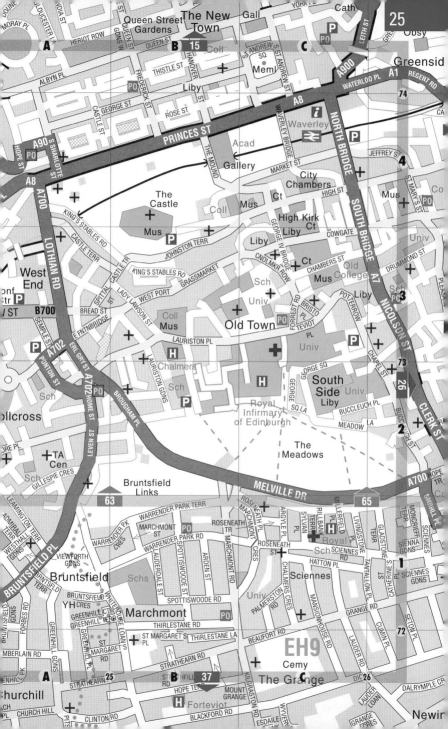

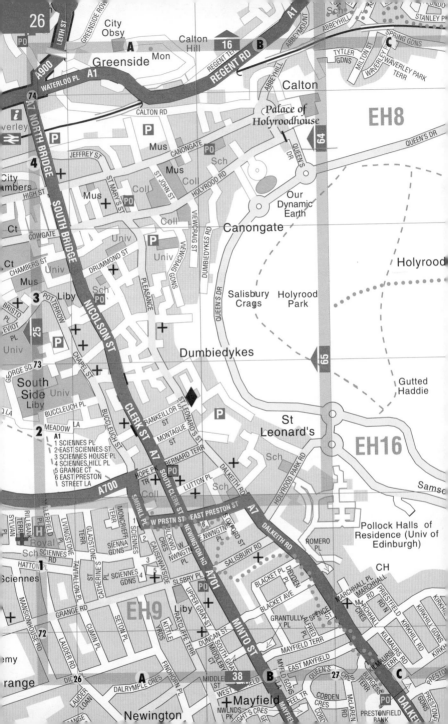

Firth of Forth

RATHBONE PL
NEW TOWER PL
IGGATE LA
IGGATE ST
BEACH LA
BANKS
MARY'S
FIELD
WILSON
PK
BATH PL
A
BATH ST
Sch

B **19**

C

74

4

TOBELLO HIGH ST

REGENT ST
REGENT ST
MARLBOROUGH ST
STRAITON PL
BELLFIELD ST
BELLFIELD TERR
BELLFIELD ST
PITVILLE STREET LA
PITVILLE ST
JOHN STREET LA W
ELCHO TERR
JOHN ST
JOHN STREET LA
LAING TERR
JAMES ST
LARRAN PL

PROMENADE

1 JOHN STREET LA E
2 JOHN STREET LA
3 JAMES STREET LA
4 LOWER JOPPA

MOUNT LODGE
WINDSOR PL
HOPE LANE N
ST MARK'S PL

ABERCORN TERR

1
2
3

BRUNSTANE RD N
BEDFORD TERR
ORMELIE TERR

4

ESPLANADE TERR

JOPPA PK

ARRY LAUDER RD

bello

ST MARK'S LA

ST MARY'S LA
ST MARY'S PL
ST MARY'S PL LA
ARGYLE CRES

JOPPA RD

PO

B6415

MUSSELBURGH

Hope Lane

A1 Ind Pk

DALKEITH ST

BRUNSTANE RD

JOPPA GR
JOPPA GDNS
JOPPA TERR

WOODSIDE TERR

Joppa

COLLESDENE DR

COLLESDENE GR

SEAVIEW CRES

SEA
T

MILTON TERR

3

EH15

CHRISTIAN CRES
CHRISTIAN GR
HOPE LA
BRAND DR
BRAND GDNS

BRUNSTANE GDNS

BRUNSTANE GARDENS MEWS

SOUTH MORTON ST
MORTON ST

COLLESDENE CRES

QUEEN'S BAY CRES

COLLESDENE AVE
COLLESDENE TERR
COLLESDENE GDNS

MILTON DR
COLLESDENE LOAN

MILTON GR

A1

MILT

DUDDINGSTON
MAINS COTTS

MILTON RD

A1

A199

A199

L Ctr

MILTON ROAD E

Cem

73

A199

Magdalene

STON
BAILIE CRES
BAILIE PL
MAGDALENE AVE
BAILIE GR
MAGDALENE PL
MAGDALENE DR
MEDWAY
MAGDALENE LOAN
MAGDALENE GDNS

PO

A1 MILTON LINK

BRUNSTANE ROAD S

Jewel & Esk
Valley Coll

BRUNSTANE BANK
BRUNSTANE CRES

30

2

DALENE
CT

Niddrie Burn

Brunstane
Prim Sch

BRUNSTANE DR

Brunstane

DAICHES BRAES

Brunstane Burn

GILBERSTOUN PL
BRUNSTANE RD S
GILBERSTOUN

Brunstane

TH GREENS
HOSIE RIGG
THE JEWEL

CORBIESHOT

CORBIEWYND

VEXHIM PK

Hypermarket

GILBERSTOUN BRAE

GILBERSTOUN LOAN
GILBERSTOUN WYND

1

Wantor
Walls

SOUTH
PARROTSHOT

Cleikimin

EH21

EKIM RD

PEACOCKTAIL CL

BLACKCHAPEL CL
BLACKCHAPEL RD

Kinnaird Pk

A1

Newcraighall
Bsns Pk

KLONDYKE ST

PO

WHITEHILL ST

72

Ne

A6095

Newcrai
Prim S

A
31
QUARRY
COTTS

B **41**

C

32

NIDRIE
COTTS

NEWCRAIGHALL RD

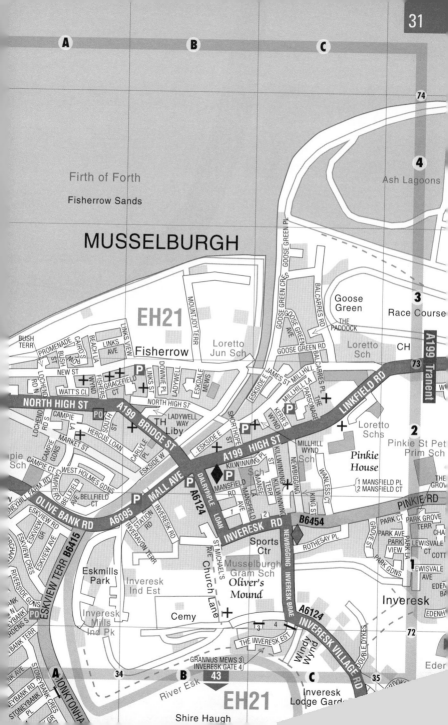

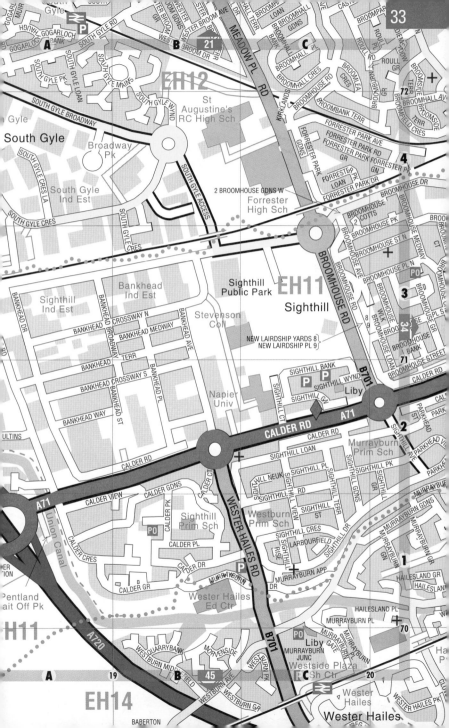

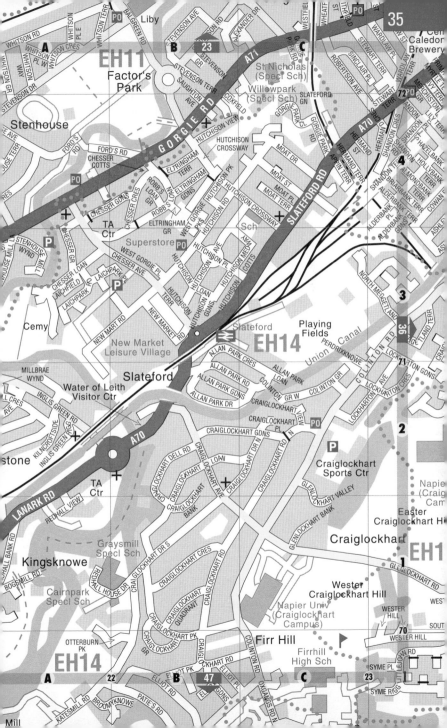

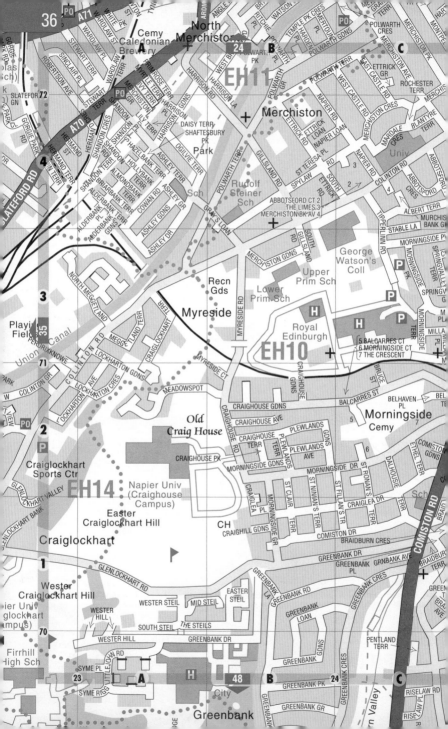

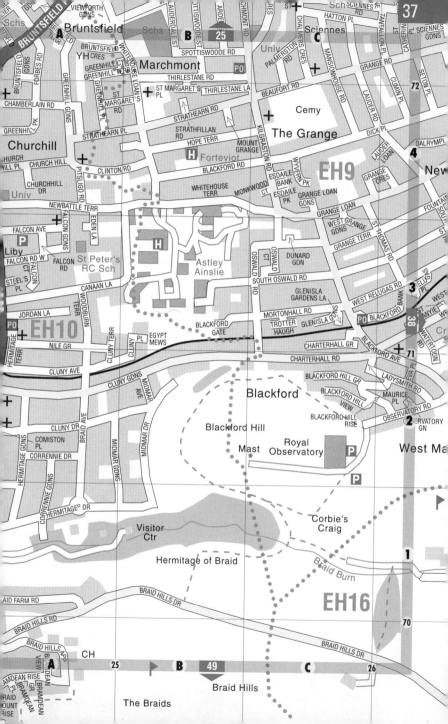

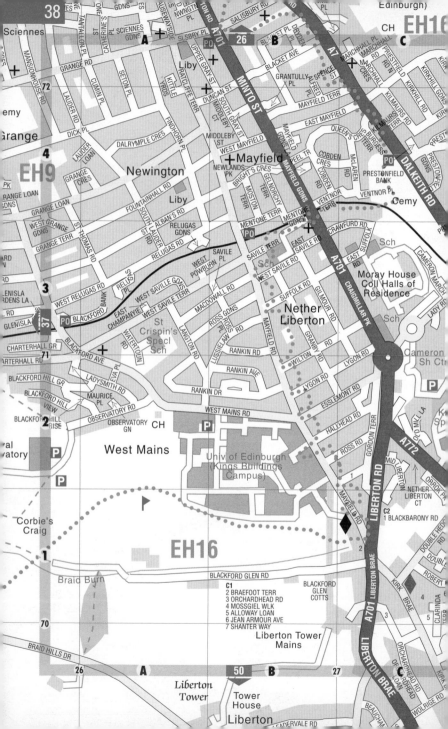

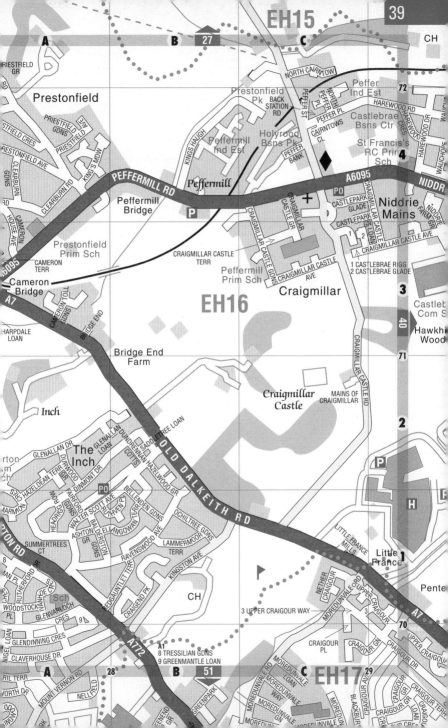

40

Braid Burn — EH15

Bingham Way

Bingham

Bingham Bro

A

28

B

Bingham Medwd

C

NIDDRIE MAINS TERR

NIDDRIE MAINS CT

NIDDRIE MILL CRES

NIDDRIE MILL PL

RTH CAIRNTOW

72

Peffer Ind Est

NIDDRIE MAINS TERR

HAY GDNS

HAY DR

NIDDRIE MAINS DR

NIDDRIE MILL DR

NIDDRIE MILL TERR

HAREWOOD RD

WAUCHOPE AVE

WAUCHOPE TERR

HAY RD

HAY PL

HAY AVE

Sch

NIDDRIE MILL GR

PEFFER ST

PEFFER PL

Castlebrae Bsns Ctr

HAREWOOD DR

WAUCHOPE CRES

NIDDRIE MAINS DR

WAUCHOPE SQ

Sch

4

St Francis's RC Prim Sch

WAUCHOPE PL

WAUCHOPE CRES

NIDDRIE MAINS RD

NIDDRIE MAINS RD

PO

A6095

NIDDRIE MAINS RD

Liby

Hays Com Bsns Ctr

NIDDRIE MARISCHAL GR

Niddrie M

CASTLEPARK GLADE

CASTLEMILLAR CASTLE GN

Niddrie Mains

NIDDRIE FARM GR

QUEEN'S WLK

CHAPEL CT

NIDDRIE MARISCHAL PL

NIDDRIE MARISCHAL RD

NIDDRIE MARISCHAL CRES

NIDDRIE

CASTLEPARK LOAN

CRAIGMILLAR CASTLE AVE

WEST CT

EAST CT

GREENDYKES AVE

NIDDRIE MARISCHAL DR

NIDDRIE HOUSE PK

NIDDRIE HOUSE DR

*1

Park

1 GREAT CARLET
2 NIDRIE HOUSE
3 NIDRIE HOUSE
4 GREAT CARLET
6 NIDRIE HOUSE

MILLAR CASTLE AVE

ALMOND CT

Greendykes

GREENDYKES DR

Sch

aigmill 3

Castlebrae Com Sch

GREENDYKES TERR

PO

Niddrie Marischal

Hawkhill Wood

39

GREENDYKES GDNS

71

CRAIGMILLAR CASTLE RD

GREENDYKES RD

B4
1 NIDDRIE MAINS DR
2 NIDDRIE MARISCHAL ST
3 NIDDRIE MARISCHAL GDNS
4 NIDDRIE MARISCHAL LOAN

MAINS OF CRAIGMILLAR

Niddrie Burn

B3
5 NIDDRIE MARISCHAL DR
6 NIDDRIE MARISCHAL GN
7 NIDDRIE HOUSE AVE
8 GREENDYKES LOAN

2

EH16

EH2

P

P

H

Edmonstone

LITTLE FRANCE MILLS

Little France

Royal Infirmary of Edinburgh

1

NETHER CRAIGOUR

MOREDUNVALE RD

UPPER CRAIGOUR

OLD DALKEITH RD

Pentecox

70

CRAIGOUR PL

CRAIGOUR GN

UPPER CRAIGOUR

Edmonstone

EH17

29

CRAIGOUR DR

CRAIGOUR TERR

CRAIGOUR GDNS

A

52

B

A7

30

C

STEW

BLACKBURN

MOREDUNVALE

CRAIGOUR AVE

CRAIGOUR GR

CRAIGOUR LOAN

CRAIGOUR CRES

OLD

THE WISP

BAC

THE WISP

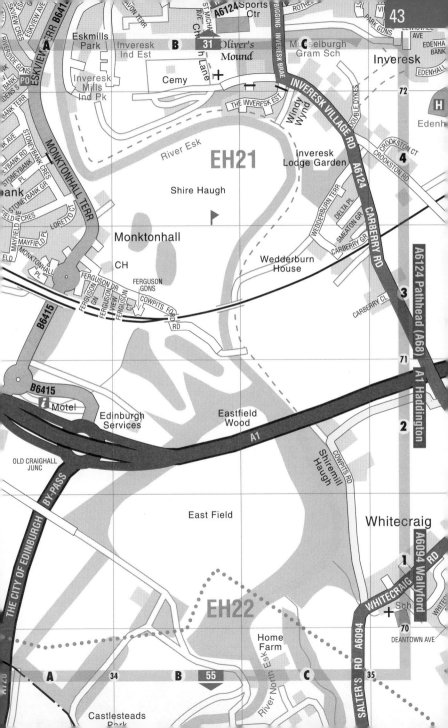

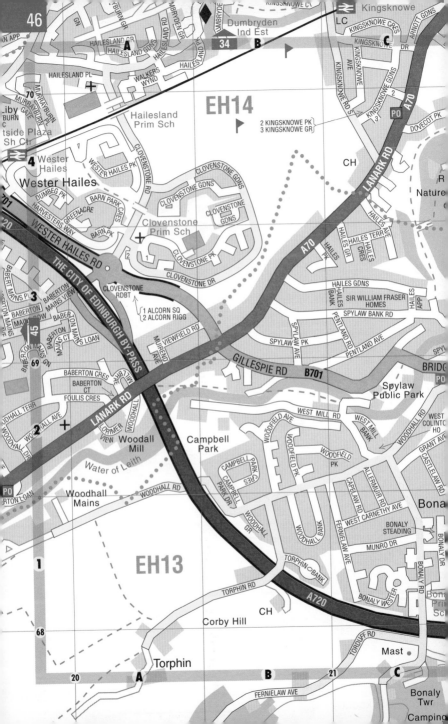

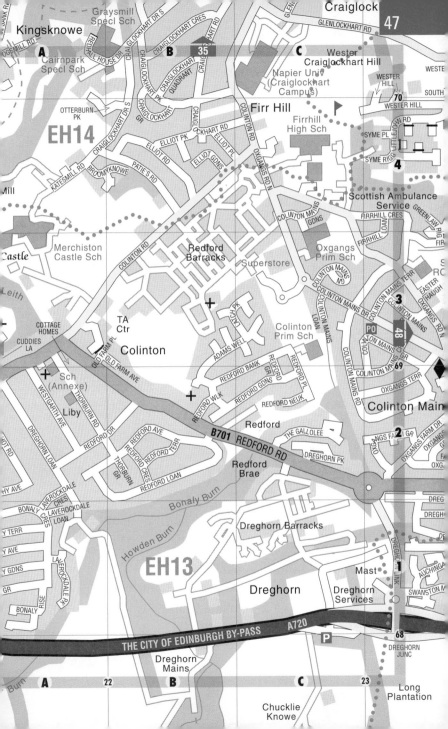

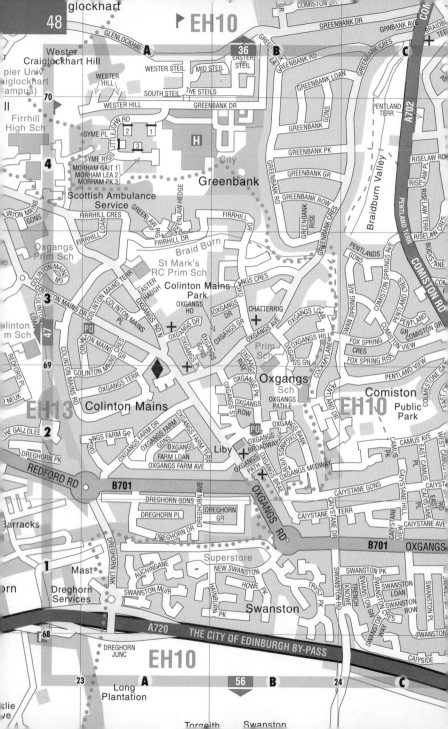

50

Braid Burn

A BLACKFORD GLEN RD 38 B

BLACKFORD GLEN COTTS

C

ROBER

DOUBL

DOUB

C4
2 BEAUCHAMP GR
3 HAWKHEAD GR
4 CLARINDA TERR

A701

70

BRAID HILLS DR

Liberton Tower Mains

CLARINDA

4

LIBERTON BRAE

ORCHARDHEAD LOAN

ORCHARDHEAD

KIRK BRAE

WOLRIGE R

4

Liberton Tower

Tower House

CLACKMAE GR 1
LEADERVALE TERR 2
KEDSLIE PL 3

LEADERVALE RD

1   2

Liberton

CLACKMAE RD

KEDSLIE RD

3

BEAUCHAMP CRES

HAWKHEAD RD

3

Cem

Tower Farm

LIBERTON DR

CADOGAN RD

Riding School

Liberton House

LIBERTON DR

PO

EH16

Liberton Kennels

ALNWICKHILL RD

Park

LIBERTON GDNS

LIBERTON DR

Meadowhead

Alnwickhill House

Wks

3

49

69

STANEDYKEHEAD

TA Ctr

Resr
2 BACKLEE

ST KATHARINE'S

ALNWICKHILL GDNS

2

Alnwickhill

NETHERBANK VIEW

NETHERBANK

ALNWICKHILL VIEW

ALNWICKHILL TERR

ALNWICKHILL DR

ALNWICKHILL PK

ST KATHARINE'S BRAE

ALNWICKHILL CT

ALNWICKHILL LOAN

HOWDEN HALL LOAN

ALNWICKHILL GR

ALNWICKHILL CRES

2

HOWDEN HALL DR

RAE'S C

HOWDEN HALL CT

HOWDEN HALL PK

HOWDEN HALL CRES

HOWDEN HALL GDNS

HOWDEN HALL DR

HOWDEN HALL RD

MORTONHALL GATE

HOWDEN HALL WAY

Crem

Kaimes

Cemy

BALMW

Mortonhall

Cemy

MORTONHALL PARK AVE

MORTONHALL PARK VIEW

3

MORTONHALL PK DR

4

MORTONHALL PK CRES

BALMM

BRAC

LY LOAN

M CL

1

MORTONHALL PARK WAY

1   2   3

MORTONHALL PARK GDNS

5

4

MORTONHALL

68

FROGSTON RD W   FROGSTON BRAE   B701   FROGSTON RD E

MORTONHALL PARK GR 1
MORTONHALL PARK LOAN 2
MORTONHALL PARK GN 3

MORTONHALL PARK TERR 3
MORTONHALL PARK BANK 4
MORTONHALL PARK PL 5

26   A   58   B   27   C

EH10

EH17

B701 OXGANGS RD

Superstore

NEW SWANSTON

48

Swanston

SWANSTON PK
SWANSTON KNOWE
SWANSTON GN
SWANSTON LOAN
SWANSTON C
SWANSTON VIEW
SWANSTON ROW
SWANSTON PL
SWAN
SWANSTON CRES
SWANSTON WAY
SWANSTON AVE

Mast

Dreghorn
Services

DREGHORN LINK
AUCHINGANE
SWANSTON MUIR
HAINBURN PK
TRUST PK
SWANSTON PK

A

B

C

720

68

DREGHORN
JUNC

THE CITY OF EDINBURGH BY-PASS

A720

CAIYSIDE

4

Long
Plantation

Torgeith
Knowe

Swanston
Cottage

SWANSTON RD

reghorn
e Ranges

EH10

CH

Swanston

thy
gh

Shearie
Knowe

Hare Burn

Swanston Burn

3

Todhole
Knowe

67

Middle
Knowe

2

Muilieputchie

White
Hill

P

Midlothian
Ski Ctr

Byerside
Hill

1

Windy Door
Nick

Caerketton
Craigs

66

Caerketton
Hill

Boghall Burn

23

A

B

24

C

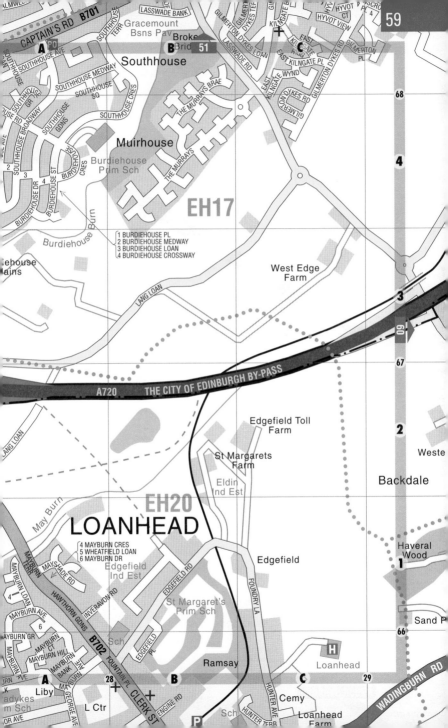

South Farm

Depot
52

A **B** **C**

A772

GILMERTON R

EAST
KILNGATE
RIGG
KILNGATE PL
WYND

GILMERTON DYKES RD
GILMERTON PL

DYKES RD
GILME

68

EH17

Slag Heap

GILMERTON STATION RD

A720

4

st Edge
Farm

THE CITY OF EDINBURGH BY-PASS

Park Burn

3

Parkburn

Englands
Hill

Melville Mains

59

67

CH

d Toll
n

2

Wester Melville

LASSWADE RD

Aggregate
Plant

Backdale

EH18

Haveral
Wood

Wading Burn

WESTMILL RD 1
POLTON RD 2
WEE BRAE 3
MELVILLE VIEW 4
ELDIN PL 5

1

eld

2 GLEBE PL

LASSWADE RD

HIGH ST

EH20

Sand Pit

Wadingburn

WADINGBURN LA

2

CHURCH RD

Cemy

SCHOOL BRAE
SCHOOL

PO

66

H

Loanhead

WADINGBURN RD   A768

GREEN LA

KEVOCK RD

KEVOCK
VALE PK

WESTMILL RD

WESTMILL WYND

River North Esk

29   **A**   A768 Loanhead

B   30   **C**

emy

Eskgrove

Broo

Loanhead
Farm

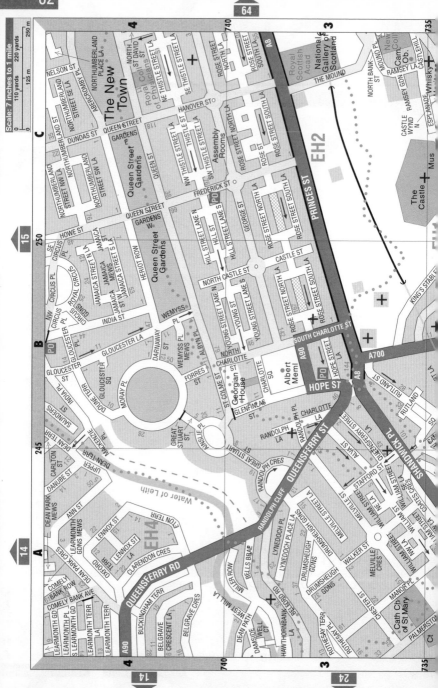

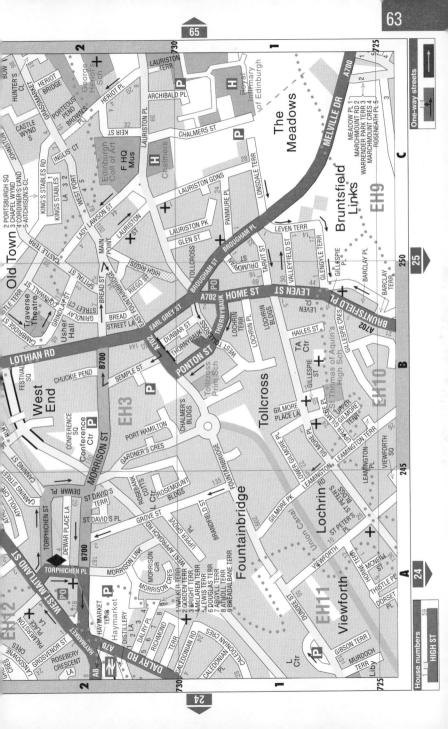

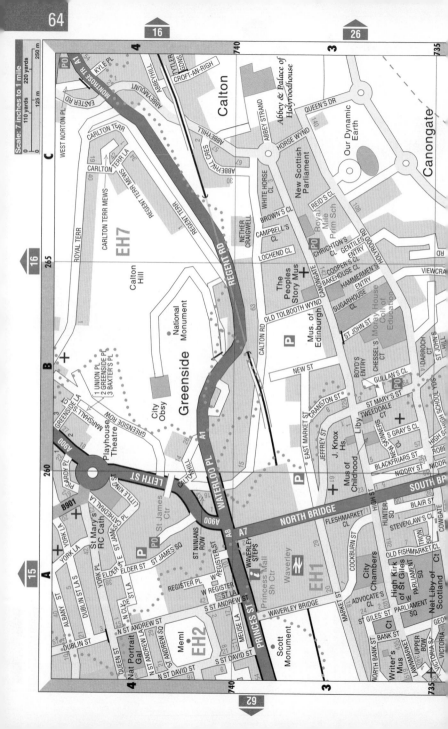

Scale: 7 inches to 1 mile

0   110 yards   220 yards
0   125 m   250 m

16
26

Calton

Canongate

Abbey & Palace of Holyroodhouse

QUEEN'S DR

Our Dynamic Earth

New Scottish Parliament

EASTER RD

KYLE PL

MONTROSE TR

A1

ABBEYMOUNT

ABBEYHILL

CUTLER GDNS

CROFT-AN-RIGH

WEST NORTON PL

CARLTON TERR

CARLTON TERR LA

CARLTON

REGENT TERR MEWS

CARLTON TERR MEWS

ABBEYHILL CRES

ABBEYHILL ST

ROYAL TERR

EH7

REGENT TERR

WHITE HORSE CL

ABBEY STRAND

HORSE WYND

REID'S CL

Royal Mile Prim Sch

BROWN'S CL

CAMPBELL'S CL

CHRICHTON'S CL

GENTILES ENTRY

HOLYROOD RD

Calton Hill

National Monument

NETHER CRAIGWELL

LOCHEND CL

CANONGATE

BAKEHOUSE CL

HAMMERMEN'S ENTRY

COOPER'S CL

SUGARHOUSE CL

The Peoples Story Mus

Mus. of Edinburgh

CHESSEL'S CT

Moray House Coll of Education

VIEWCRA

RD

Greenside

City Obsy

Playhouse Theatre

1 UNION PL
2 GREENSIDE PL
3 BAXTER'S PL

GREENSIDE LA

GREENSIDE ROW

GREENSIDE ROW

MARSHALL'S CT

CALTON HILL

REGENT RD

WATERLOO PL

CALTON RD

OLD TOLBOOTH WYND

NEW ST

BOYD'S ENTRY

GULLAN'S CL

ST JOHN ST

DARROCH CT

ST JOHN'S HILL

A1

EAST MARKET ST

CRANSTON ST

JEFFREY ST

J. Knox Hs.

Liby

ST MARY'S ST

TWEEDDALE CT

S GRAY'S CL

SKINNERS CL

HIGH SCHOOL YDS

ROBE

NIDDR

LEITH ST

ST ANDREW SQ

PICARDY PL

B901

ST JAMES CTR

CATHEDRAL LA

LITTLE KING ST

St Mary's RC Cath

LEOPOLD PL

BROUGHTON ST LA

YORK LA

YORK PL

ELDER ST

ST JAMES SQ

ST NINIANS ROW

BLACKFRIARS ST

NIDDRY ST

Mus. of Childhood

SOUTH BR

HIGH ST

A7

A8

A900

NORTH BRIDGE

FLESHMARKET CL

BLAIR ST

HUNTER SQ

STEVENLAW'S CL

OLD FISHMARKET CL

COWGATE

EH1

ALBANY ST

DUBLIN ST LA S

DUBLIN ST

YORK PL

ELDER ST

REGISTER PL

W REGISTER ST

S ST ANDREW ST

N ST ANDREW ST

REGISTER ST

PO

PO

P

P

P

PO

PO

PO

Waverley

WAVERLEY STEPS

Princess Mall Sh Ctr

i

City Chambers

COCKBURN ST

MARKET ST

ADVOCATE'S CL

PARLIAMENT SQ

High Kirk of St Giles

Nat Liby of Scotland

QUEEN ST

ST ANDREW SQ

N ST ANDREW LA

S ST ANDREW ST

S ST DAVID ST

N ST DAVID ST

PRINCES ST

WAVERLEY BRIDGE

MEUSE LA

Meml

EH2

Nat Portrait Gal

Scott Monument

St Giles' St

ST GILES' CL

BANK ST

NORTH BANK ST

Writer's Mus

LAWNMARKET

UPPER BOW

VICTORIA ST

VICTORIA TERR

GEO

735
740
260
265

15
16

3
3

62

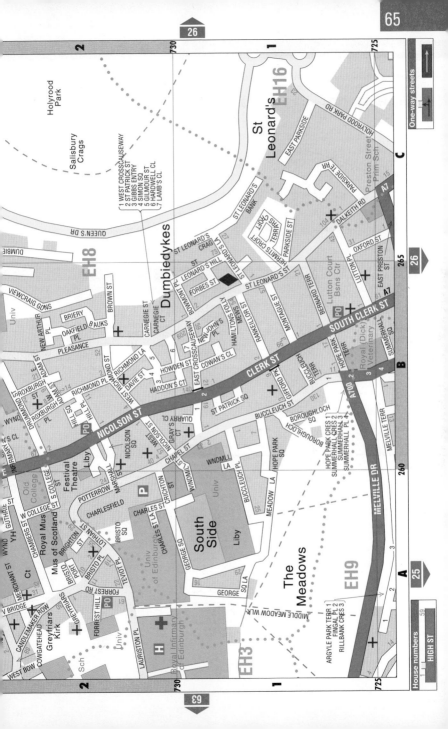

Holyrood Park

Salisbury Crags

QUEEN'S DR

DUMBIE

EH8

Dumbiedykes

St Leonard's

EH16

1 WEST CROSSCAUSEWAY
2 ST PATRICK ST
3 GIBBS ENTRY
4 SIMON SQ
5 GILMOUR ST
6 HARDWELL CL
7 LAMB'S CL

VIEWCRAIG GDNS

Univ

BROWN ST

BRIERY BAUKS
OAKFIELD PL
PLEASANCE
NEW ARTHUR PL

CARNEGIE ST
CARNEGIE CT

ST LEONARD'S CRAG
ST LEONARD'S HILL
ST LEONARD'S BANK
ST LEONARD'S LANE

BOWMONT PL
FORBES ST

ST LEONARD'S ST

HERMITS CROFT
PARKSIDE TERR
PARKSIDE ST

EAST PARKSIDE

PARKSIDE TERR

Preston Street Prim Sch

DALKEITH RD

OXFORD ST

EAST PRESTON ST

A7

ROXBURGH PL
ROXBURGH ST
ADAM ST
DRUMMOND ST
HILL SQ
HILL PL
RICHMOND PL

RICHMOND LA
WEST RICHMOND ST
DAVIE ST
HOWDEN LA
HADDON'S CT

NEW JOHN'S PL
HAMILTON'S FOLLY MEWS
RANKEILLOR ST
MONTAGUE ST
BERNARD TERR

Lutton Court Bsns Ctr
LUTTON PL

104

SUMMERHALL
Royal (Dick) Veterinary

SUMMERHALL SQ

WYND
ST MARY'S CL
INFIRMARY ST

Festival Theatre

Liby

NICOLSON SQ
NICOLSON ST

WEST NICOLSON ST
GRAY'S CT
QUARRY CL
CHAPEL ST

NICOLSON ST

ST PATRICK SQ

EAST CROSSCAUSEWAY
ST LEONARD'S ST

CLERK ST

SOUTH CLERK ST

BUCCLEUCH ST
GIFFORD PARK
BUCCLEUCH TERR
HOPE PARK TERR

A7

265

A7

GUTHRIE ST
MERCHANT ST
Ct
CHAMBERS ST
Royal Mus
Mus of Scotland
Old College
Univ
College

W COLLEGE ST
S COLLEGE ST

CHARLESFIELD
POTTERROW
MARSHALL ST
CRICHTON ST
WINDMILL LA
WNDMLL

BUCCLEUCH PL
HOPE PARK SQ

BOROUGHLOCH SQ
BOROUGHLOCH

HOPE PARK CRES 1
SUMMERHALL CRES 2
SUMMERHALL 3
SUMMERHALL PL 4

MELVILLE TERR

LOTHIAN ST
BRISTO PL
BRIGHTON ST
BRISTO PORT
BRISTO ST
TEVIOT PL
FORREST RD

CHARLES ST
CHARLES ST LA

GEORGE SQ

CHARLESFIELD

BRISTO SQ

Univ of Edinburgh

South Side

Liby

Univ

GEORGE SQ LA
GEORGE SQ

MEADOW LA

MELVILLE DR

The Meadows

MIDDLE MEADOW WLK

ARGYLE PARK TERR 1
FINGAL PL 2
RILLBANK CRES 3

EH9

EH3

V BRIDGE
COWGATEHEAD
CANDLEMAKER ROW
GREYFRIARS
Greyfriars Kirk
WEST BOW

Royal Infirmary of Edinburgh

Univ
Sch
LAURISTON PL
FORREST HILL
YH
W GUTHRIE ST

H

26
25
730
725
260
725
730
63

House numbers
HIGH ST
One-way streets

Index

Street names are listed alphabetically and show the locality, the Postcode District, the page number and a reference to the square in which the name falls on the map page

Queen's Ave 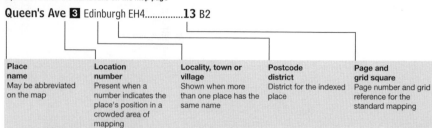 Edinburgh EH4...............13 B2

Place name
May be abbreviated on the map

Location number
Present when a number indicates the place's position in a crowded area of mapping

Locality, town or village
Shown when more than one place has the same name

Postcode district
District for the indexed place

Page and grid square
Page number and grid reference for the standard mapping

Public and commercial buildings are highlighted in magenta. **Places of interest** are highlighted in blue with a star★

Abbreviations used in the index

Acad	**Academy**	Comm	**Common**	Gd	**Ground**	L	**Leisure**	Prom	**Prom**
App	**Approach**	Cott	**Cottage**	Gdn	**Garden**	La	**Lane**	Rd	**Road**
Arc	**Arcade**	Cres	**Crescent**	Gn	**Green**	Liby	**Library**	Recn	**Recreation**
Ave	**Avenue**	Cswy	**Causeway**	Gr	**Grove**	Mdw	**Meadow**	Ret	**Retail**
Bglw	**Bungalow**	Ct	**Court**	H	**Hall**	Meml	**Memorial**	Sh	**Shopping**
Bldg	**Building**	Ctr	**Centre**	Ho	**House**	Mkt	**Market**	Sq	**Square**
Bsns, Bus	**Business**	Ctry	**Country**	Hospl	**Hospital**	Mus	**Museum**	St	**Street**
Bvd	**Boulevard**	Cty	**County**	HQ	**Headquarters**	Orch	**Orchard**	Sta	**Station**
Cath	**Cathedral**	Dr	**Drive**	Hts	**Heights**	Pal	**Palace**	Terr	**Terrace**
Cir	**Circus**	Dro	**Drove**	Ind	**Industrial**	Par	**Parade**	TH	**Town Hall**
Cl	**Close**	Ed	**Education**	Inst	**Institute**	Pas	**Passage**	Univ	**University**
Cnr	**Corner**	Emb	**Embankment**	Int	**International**	Pk	**Park**	Wk, Wlk	**Walk**
Coll	**College**	Est	**Estate**	Intc	**Interchange**	Pl	**Place**	Wr	**Water**
Com	**Community**	Ex	**Exhibition**	Junc	**Junction**	Prec	**Precinct**	Yd	**Yard**

Index of localities, towns and villages

Abbeyhill 16 C1
Alnwickhill 50 A2
Baberton 45 B3
Barnton 11 A3
Beaverbank 15 C4
Bingham 28 B2
Blackford 37 C2
Blackhall 12 C2
Bonaly 46 C1
Bonnington 15 C4
Bonnyrigg 61 B1
Braepark 11 A3
Broomhouse 34 A3
Broughton 15 C2
Brunstane 29 C2
Bruntsfield 25 A1
Bruntsfield Links ...63 C1
Bughtlin 10 C1
Calton 16 B1
Calton 64 C4
Cammo 10 B2
Canongate 64 C3
Canonmills 15 B2
Carrick Knowe 22 C1
Churchill 37 A4
Claremont Park ...17 B4
Cleikimin 29 A1
Clermiston 11 C1

Coates 24 B3
Colinton 47 B3
Colinton Mains ...48 A2
Comely Bank 14 B2
Corslet 44 C2
Corstorphine 22 B2
Craigentinny 17 C2
Craigleith 14 A2
Craiglockhart 35 C1
Craigmillar 39 C3
Cramond 3 B1
Cramond Bridge ..10 B3
Dalry 24 B2
Danderhall 53 B3
Davidson's Mains ..12 A3
Dean 14 B1
Dreghorn 47 C1
Drum 16 C2
Drumbrae 11 A2
Drylaw 13 B3
Duddingston 28 A2
Dumbiedykes 65 B2
East Craigs 21 A3
East Hermiston ..32 C1
Easter Millerhill ..54 A4
Edinburgh 25 C2
Edmonstone 40 B1
Eskbank 61 C2

Factor's Park 23 B1
Fairmilehead 49 A1
Ferniehill 52 A3
Firr Hill 47 C4
Fisherrow 31 B3
Fountainbridge ..63 A1
Gayfield 16 A2
Gilmerton 52 B2
Goldenacre 15 A4
Gorgie 23 C1
Gracemount 51 A1
Granton 6 A3
Greenbank 48 B4
Greendykes 40 B3
Greenside 16 A1
Greenside 64 B4
Hermiston 32 B1
Hermitage 17 A3
Hillside 16 B2
Holyrood 26 C3
Inverleith 14 C4
Jock's Lodge 17 C1
Joppa 29 C3
Juniper Green ...45 B2
Kingsknowe 35 A1
Lasswade 61 B1
Leith 9 B2
Liberton 50 B4

Loanhead 59 A1
Lochend 17 A2
Lochrin 63 A1
Longstone 34 A2
Magdalene 29 A2
Marchmont 25 B1
Mayfield 38 B4
Meadowbank 17 A2
Merchiston 36 B4
Monktonhall 43 B3
Moredun 51 C4
Morningside 36 C2
Mortonhall 50 A1
Muirhouse 5 A2
Murrayfield 23 A3
Musselburgh 31 A3
Myreside 36 A3
Nether Liberton ..38 B3
Newcraighall 42 A4
Newhailes 30 C2
Newhaven 7 C2
Newington 38 A4
Newton Village ..53 C3
Niddrie 40 C3
Niddrie Mains 40 A4
Niddrie Mill 40 C4
North Leith 8 A2
North Merchiston ..24 A1

Old Craighall 42 C2
Old Pentland 58 B1
Old Town 63 B2
Orchard Brae 14 A1
Oxgangs 48 B2
Parkhead 34 B2
Piershill 18 A1
Pilrig 16 A4
Pilton 6 A1
Port of Leith 8 A4
Portobello 28 B4
Prestonfield 39 A4
Quarryholes 16 C3
Ravelston 23 A4
Restalrig 17 C2
Riccarton 44 A3
Roseburn 23 C3
St Leonard's 65 C1
Saughton 22 C2
Saughton 34 B4
Seafield 17 C4
Sighthill 33 C3
Siverknowes 4 A1
Slateford 35 B2
South Gyle 33 A4
South Leith 8 C1
South Side 65 A1
Southhouse 51 B1

Stenhouse 35 A4
Stockbridge 14 C2
Stoneybank 42 C4
Swanston 48 B1
Swanston 56 C3
The Grange 37 C4
The Gyle 21 A2
The Inch 39 A2
The New Town ...62 C4
Tollcross 63 B1
Trinity 7 B1
Viewforth 63 A1
Wardie 6 C2
Warriston 15 B4
West Craigs 20 B3
West End 63 B2
West Mains 38 A2
West Pilton 5 B1
Wester Hailes ...45 C4
Wester Millerhill ..54 A3
Whitecraig 43 C1
Willowbrae 27 B3

A

1 Ind Pk EH15 ....29 C3
bbey and Palace of
Holyroodhouse★
obeyhill 64 C3
obeyhill
  Edinburgh EH8 .....16 C1
obeyhill Crt 64 C4
obeyhill Cres EH8 ....64 C4
  EH7 ....16 C1
obey La EH8 ....64 C1
obeymount EH8 ....64 C4
obey St EH7 ....16 C1
obey Strand EH8 .....64 C3
obbotsford Cres
  EH10 ....36 C4
bbotsford Ct EH10 ...36 C4
bercorn Ave EH8 .....27 C4
bercorn Ct EH8 ......27 C3
bercorn Dr EH8 ......27 B4
bercorn Gdns EH8 ...17 C1
bercorn Gr EH8 ......27 B4
bercorn Rd
  G Edinburgh EH8 ...17 B1
bercorn Terr EH8 ....27 B4
bercorn Terr EH15 ...29 A4
bercromby Pl EH3 ...62 C4
binger Gdns EH12 ...23 C3
cademy Pk EH6 ......16 C4
cademy St EH6 ......16 C4
dams Well EH13 .....47 B3
delphi Gr
  Edinburgh EH15 ....18 C1
delphi Pl EH15 ......28 C4
dmiral Terr EH10 ....25 A1
dmiralty St EH6 .....08 B2
dvocate's Cl EH1 ....64 A3
ffleck Ct EH12 ......20 C4
fton Pl EH5 ....06 C1
fton Terr EH5 ....06 C1
gnew Terr EH6 ......07 C1
inslie Pl EH3 ....62 B4
itchison's Cl EH1 ...63 C2
itchison's Pl EH15 ..18 C1
an Breck Gdns
  Edinburgh EH1 .....21 C4
  EH4 ....11 C1
lbany La EH1 ....15 C1
lbany St EH1 ....64 A4
lbert Rd EH6 ....09 A1
lbert St EH7 ....16 B3
lbert Terr EH10 .....36 C4
lbion Bsns Ctr EH8 .16 C2
lbion Pl EH7 ....16 C2
lbion Terr EH7 ......16 C2
lbyn Pl EH2 ....62 B4
lcorn Rigg EH14 ....46 A3
lcorn Sq EH14 ......46 A3
lderbank Gdns
  EH11 ....36 A4
lderbank Pl EH11 ...36 A4
lderbank Terr EH11 .36 A4
lemoor Cres EH17 ..43 A4
lemoor Pk EH7 .....17 A3
lexander Dr EH11 ..23 B1
lfred Pl
  Edinburgh EH9 ....26 B1
  EH8 ....38 B4
llanfield EH7 ....16 B2
llan Pk Cres EH14 ..35 B3
llan Pk Dr EH14 ....35 B2
llan Pk Gdns EH14 .35 B2
llan Pk Ln EH14 ....35 B2
llan Pk Rd EH14 ....35 B2
llan St EH14 ....14 C2
llermuir Rd EH13 ...46 C2
lloway Loan 5
  EH16 ....38 C1
lmond Bank Cotts
  EH4 ....03 A1
lmondbank Terr
  EH11 ....36 A4
lmond Ct EH16 ......40 A3
lmond Ct E EH16 ...40 A3
lmond Ct W EH4 ....10 C3
lmond Gn EH12 .....20 C4
lmond Sq EH12 .....20 C4
lnwickhill Cres
  EH16 ....50 B2
lnwickhill Ct EH16 .50 B2
lnwickhill Dr EH16 .50 B2
lnwickhill Gdns
  EH16 ....50 B2
lnwickhill Gr EH16 .50 B2
lnwickhill Loan
  EH16 ....50 B2
lnwickhill Pk EH16 .50 C2
lnwickhill Rd EH16 .50 C2
lnwickhill Terr
  EH16 ....50 B2
lnwickhill View
  EH16 ....50 B2
lva Pl EH7 ....16 C2

Alva St EH2 ....62 A3
Anderson Pl EH6 ....08 A1
Andrew Wood Ct
  EH6 ....07 B2
Angle Pk Terr EH11 ....24 B1
Angres Ct EH22 ....53 B3
Annandale St EH7 ......16 A2
Annandale St La EH7 ...16 A2
Annfield EH6 ....07 C2
Annfield St EH6 ....07 C2
Ann St EH4 ....62 A4
Antigua St 7 EH1 ......16 A2
Appin Terr EH14 ....35 C4
Arboretum Ave EH4 ....14 C2
Arboretum Pl EH3 .....14 C3
Arboretum Rd EH3 ....14 C3
Archibald Pl EH3 .....63 C2
Arden St EH9 ....25 B1
Ardmillan Pl EH11 ....24 B1
Ardmillan Terr EH11 ..24 A1
Ardshiel Ave
  Edinburgh EH12 .....21 C4
Argyle Cres EH15 .....29 B3
Argyle Pk Terr EH9 ...65 A1
Argyle Pl EH9 ....25 B1
Argyll Terr EH11 .....63 A2
Arnott Gdns EH14 .....34 C1
Arran Pl EH15 ....29 B4
Arthur St EH6 ....16 B3
Arthur St La EH6 .....16 B3
Arthur View Cres
  EH22 ....53 A4
Arthur View Terr
  EH22 ....53 A4
Ashley Dr EH11 ....36 A3
Ashley Gr EH11 ....36 A3
Ashley Pl EH6 ....16 A4
Ashley Terr EH11 .....36 A3
Ashton Gr EH16 ......39 A1
Ashville Terr EH6 ....16 C3
Assembly Rooms★
  EH2 ....62 C4
Assembly St EH6 ......08 C1
Astley Ainslie Hospl
  EH9 ....37 B3
Atholl Cres EH3 ......63 A2
Atholl Cres La EH3 ...63 A2
Atholl Terr EH3 ......63 A2
Auchingane EH10 .....48 A1
Auchinleck Ct EH6 ...07 B2
Avenue Villas EH4 ....14 A2
Avondale Pl EH3 .....15 A2
Avon Gr EH4 ....10 C4
Avon Pl EH4 ....10 C4
Avon Rd EH4 ....10 C4

B

Babert Mains Pl
  EH14 ....45 B3
Baberton Ave EH14 ...45 C2
Baberton Cres EH14 ..45 C2
Baberton Ct EH14 ....46 A2
Baberton Loan EH14 ..45 C1
Baberton Mains
  EH14 ....45 B4
Baberton Mains Ave
  EH14 ....45 C3
Baberton Mains Bank
  EH14 ....45 C3
Baberton Mains Brae
  EH14 ....45 B3
Baberton Mains Cres
  EH14 ....45 C3
Baberton Mains Ct
  EH14 ....45 C3
Baberton Mains Dell
  EH14 ....45 C3
Baberton Mains Dr
  EH14 ....45 C3
Baberton Mains Gdns
  EH14 ....45 B4
Baberton Mains Gn
  EH14 ....45 C3
Baberton Mains Gr
  EH14 ....45 C3
Baberton Mains Hill
  EH14 ....45 B3
Baberton Mains Lea
  EH14 ....45 B3
Baberton Mains Loan
  EH14 ....45 B3
Baberton Mains Pk
  EH14 ....45 B3
Baberton Mains Rise
  EH14 ....45 B3
Baberton Mains Row
  EH14 ....45 C3
Baberton Mains Terr
  EH14 ....45 C3
Baberton Mains View
  EH14 ....45 C3
Baberton Mains Way
  EH14 ....45 B3

Baberton Mains Wood
  EH14 ....45 B3
Baberton Mains Wynd
  EH14 ....45 C3
Back Dean EH4 ....54 C4
Backdean Rd EH22 ...52 C4
Backlee EH16 ....50 C2
Back Sta Rd EH16 ....39 C4
Baileyfield Cres
  EH15 ....28 C4
Baileyfield Est EH15 .28 C4
Baileyfield Rd
  Edinburgh, Northfield
  EH15 ....18 B1
  Edinburgh, Portobello
  EH15 ....28 C4
Bailie Gr EH15 ....29 A2
Bailie Path EH15 .....28 C2
Bailie Pl EH15 ....29 A2
Bailie Terr EH15 .....28 C2
Baird Ave EH12 ....23 B2
Baird Dr EH12 ....23 B2
Baird Gdns EH12 .....23 B2
Baird Gr EH12 ....23 B2
Baird Terr EH12 ......23 B2
Bakehouse Cl EH8 ....64 B3
Balbirnie Pl EH12 ....24 A2
Balcarres Ct EH10 ...36 C2
Balcarres Pl EH21 ...31 C3
Balcarres Rd EH21 ...31 C3
Balcarres St EH10 ...36 C1
Balderston Gdns
  EH16 ....39 A1
Balfour Ct EH11 ......11 A1
Balfour Pl EH6 ....16 A4
Balfour St EH6 ....16 B4
Balfron Loan EH4 ....11 B1
Balgreen Ave EH12 ..22 C2
Balgreen Gdns EH12 .22 C2
Balgreen Pl EH12 ....22 C2
Balgreen Prim Sch
  EH11 ....23 B1
Balgreen Rd EH12 ...23 A2
Ballantyne Rd EH6 ...08 B1
Balmoral Pl EH3 .....15 A2
Balmwell Ave EH16 ..51 A1
Balmwell Gr EH16 ...51 A1
Balmwell Pl EH16 ...51 A1
Balmwell Terr EH16 ..50 C1
Baltic St EH6 ....08 C1
Bangholm Ave EH5 ..07 A1
Bangholm Bower Ave
  EH5 ....07 A1
Bangholm Gr EH5 ...07 B1
Bangholm Loan EH5 .07 B1
Bangholm Pk EH5 ...07 A1
Bangholm Pl EH5 ...07 A1
Bangholm Rd EH5 ...07 A1
Bangholm Terr EH3 ..15 A4
Bangholm View EH5 .07 B1
Bangor Rd EH6 ....08 B1
Bankhead Ave EH11 .33 B3
Bankhead Broadway
  EH11 ....33 A3
Bankhead Crossway N
  EH11 ....33 A3
Bankhead Crossway S
  EH11 ....33 A3
Bankhead Dr EH11 ...33 A3
Bankhead Ind Est
  EH11 ....33 B3
Bankhead Medway
  EH11 ....33 B2
Bankhead Pl EH11 ...33 B2
Bankhead St EH11 ...33 B2
Bankhead Terr EH11 .33 A2
Bankhead Way EH11 .33 A2
Bank St EH1 ....64 A3
Barclay Pl EH10 .....63 B1
Barclay Terr EH10 ...63 B1
Barn Pk EH14 ....46 A3
Barn Pk Cres EH14 ..46 A3
Barnshot Rd EH13 ...47 A2
Barnton Ave
  Edinburgh EH4 .....11 C4
Barnton Ave W EH4 .11 A4
Barnton Brae EH4 ...11 A4
Barnton Ct EH4 ......11 A3
Barntongate Ave
  EH4 ....11 A3
Barntongate Dr EH4 .11 A3
Barntongate Terr
  EH4 ....11 A3
Barnton Gdns EH4 ...11 B3
Barnton Gr EH4 ......11 A3
Barnton Junc EH4 ...11 A4
Barnton Loan EH4 ...11 B3
Barnton Pk EH4 ......11 B3
Barnton Pk Ave EH4 .11 B3
Barnton Pk Cres EH4 .11 B3
Barnton Pk Dell EH4 .11 B3
Barnton Pk Gdns
  EH4 ....11 B3
Barnton Pk Gr EH4 ..11 B3

Barnton Pk View
  EH4 ....11 B3
Barnton Pk Wood
  EH4 ....11 B2
Baronscourt Rd EH8 .17 B1
Baronscourt Terr
  EH8 ....17 C1
Barons Ct EH14 ......45 C4
Barony Pl 6 EH3 .....15 C2
Barony St EH3 ....15 C2
Barony Terr EH12 ....21 C3
Bathfield EH6 ....08 A2
Bath Pl EH15 ....19 A1
Bath Rd EH6 ....09 A1
Bath St EH15 ....29 A4
Bath St La EH15 .....29 A4
Baxter's Pl EH1 .....64 B4
Beach La
  Edinburgh EH15 ....19 A1
  3 Edinburgh EH15 ..28 C4
  Musselburgh EH21 ..31 A3
Beauchamp Gr 2
  EH16 ....50 C4
Beauchamp Rd EH16 .50 C4
Beaufort Rd EH9 ....25 C2
Beaverbank Bsns Pk
  EH7 ....15 B3
Beaverbank Pl EH7 ..15 B3
Beaverhall Rd EH7 ..15 C3
Bedford Ct 3 EH4 ...14 C2
Bedford St EH4 ......14 C2
Bedford Terr EH15 ..29 B4
Beech Gr Ave EH22 ..61 C1
Beechmount Cres
  EH12 ....23 A3
Beechmount Pk
  EH12 ....23 A2
Beechwood Mains
  EH12 ....22 A3
Beechwood Terr EH6 .17 A3
Belford Ave EH4 .....14 A1
Belford Gdns EH4 ...14 A1
Belford Mews EH4 ..24 B4
Belford Pk EH4 ......24 B4
Belford Rd
  Edinburgh EH4 .....24 B4
  EH4 ....62 A3
Belford Terr EH4 ....24 B4
Belgrave Cres EH4 ..62 A4
Belgrave Cres La
  EH4 ....62 A4
Belgrave Gdns EH12 .22 A3
Belgrave Pl EH4 .....14 B1
Belgrave Rd EH12 ...22 A3
Belhaven Pl EH10 ...36 C2
Belhaven Terr EH10 .36 C2
Bellenden Gdns
  EH16 ....39 B1
Bellevue EH7 ....15 C2
Bellevue Cres EH3 ..15 C2
Bellevue Gdns EH7 ..15 C3
Bellevue Gr EH7 ....15 C2
Bellevue La EH7 ....15 C2
Bellevue Pl EH7 ....15 C2
Bellevue Rd EH7 ....15 C2
Bellevue St EH7 ....15 C2
Bellevue Terr EH7 ..15 C2
Bellfield Ave EH21 ..31 A1
Bellfield Ct EH21 ...31 A1
Bellfield La EH15 ...29 A4
Bellfield St EH15 ...29 A4
Bell Pl EH3 ....15 A2
Bells Brae EH4 ......62 A3
Belmont Ave EH12 ..23 A3
Belmont Cres EH12 .23 A3
Belmont Gdns EH12 .23 A3
Belmont Pk EH12 ...23 A3
Belmont Rd EH14 ...45 C2
Belmont St EH12 ....23 A3
Belmont Terr EH12 .23 A3
Belmont View EH12 .23 A3
Belvedere Pk EH6 ...07 B2
Beresford Ave EH5 ..07 B1
Beresford Gdns EH5 .07 B1
Beresford Pl EH5 ...07 A1
Beresford Terr EH5 ..07 B2
Bernard St EH6 .....08 C2
Bernard Terr EH8 ...65 C1
Biggar Rd
  Edinburgh EH10 ....49 A1
  Edinburgh EH10 ....57 A3
Bingham Ave EH15 ..28 B1
Bingham Broadway ..28 B1
Bingham Cres EH15 .28 B1
Bingham Crossway
  EH15 ....28 B1
Bingham Dr EH15 ...28 C1
Bingham Medway
  EH15 ....28 B1
Bingham Pl EH15 ...28 B1
Bingham Pl EH15 ....28 B1
Bingham Way EH15 .28 B1
Birch Ct EH4 ....06 A2
Blackadder Pl EH4 ..06 A2
Blackbarony Rd 1
  EH16 ....38 C2
Blackburn Crag EH17 .51 C4
Blackchapel Cl EH15 .41 A4

Blackchapel Rd EH15 .41 A4
Blacket Ave EH9 .....26 B1
Blacket Pl EH9 ......26 B1
Blackford Ave EH9 ..37 C3
Blackford Bank EH9 .37 C3
Blackford Gate EH9 .37 C3
Blackford Glen Cotts
  EH17 ....38 B1
Blackford Glen Rd
  EH17 ....38 B1
Blackford Hill Gr
  EH9 ....37 C2
Blackford Hill Rise
  EH9 ....37 C2
Blackford Hill View
  EH9 ....37 C2
Blackford Rd EH9 ...37 B4
Blackfriars St EH1 ..64 B3
Blackhall Prim Sch
  EH4 ....12 C1
Blackie Rd EH6 ......16 C4
Blackthorn Ct EH4 ..11 A2
Blackwood Cres EH9 .26 A1
Blaeberry Gdns EH4 .11 A2
Blair St EH1 ....64 A3
Blandfield EH7 ......15 C3
Blantyre Terr EH10 ..37 B1
Bleachfield EH6 .....15 C4
Blinkbonny Ave EH4 .13 C1
Blinkbonny Cres EH4 .13 B1
Blinkbonny Gdns
  EH4 ....13 C1
Blinkbonny Gr EH4 ..13 C1
Blinkbonny Gr W
  EH4 ....13 C1
Blinkbonny Rd EH4 ..13 C1
Blinkbonny Terr EH4 .13 B1
Boat Gn EH3 ....15 B3
Bogpark Rd EH21 ...30 C2
Bogsmill Rd EH14 ...35 C2
Bonaly Ave EH13 ....47 A1
Bonaly Brae EH13 ...47 A1
Bonaly Cres EH13 ...47 A1
Bonaly Dr EH13 .....46 C1
Bonaly Gdns EH13 ..47 A1
Bonaly Gr EH13 .....47 A1
Bonaly Prim Sch
  EH13 ....46 C1
Bonaly Rd EH13 .....47 A2
Bonaly Rise EH13 ...47 A1
Bonaly Steading
  EH13 ....46 C1
Bonaly Terr EH13 ...47 A1
Bonaly Wester EH13 .46 C1
Bonar Pl EH6 ....07 C1
Bonnington Ave EH6 .07 C2
Bonnington Bsns Ctr
  EH6 ....16 A4
Bonnington Gr EH6 ..07 C1
Bonnington Ind Est
  EH6 ....16 A4
Bonnington Prim Sch
  EH6 ....16 A4
Bonnington Rd EH6 ..16 A4
Bonnington Rd La
  EH6 ....16 A4
Bonnington Terr EH6 .07 C2
Bonnyhaugh EH6 ....15 C4
Bonnyhaugh La EH6 .15 C4
Boothacre La EH6 ...17 B4
Boroughloch EH8 ...65 B3
Boroughloch Sq EH8 .65 B1
Boroughmuir High Sch
  EH10 ....25 A1
Boroughmuir High Sch
  Annexe EH10 ....37 A2
Boroughmuir High Sch
  (Annexe) EH11 .....24 B1
Borthwick Pl EH12 ..24 A3
Boswall Ave EH5 ....06 B1
Boswall Cres EH5 ...06 B1
Boswall Dr EH5 .....06 B2
Boswall Gdns EH5 ..06 B1
Boswall Gn EH5 .....06 B2
Boswall Gr EH5 .....06 B2
Boswall Loan EH5 ..06 B1
Boswall Parkway
  EH5 ....06 B2
Boswall Pl EH5 .....06 B2
Boswall Quad EH5 ..06 B2
Boswall Rd EH5 .....06 C2
Boswall Sq EH5 .....06 B2
Boswall Terr EH5 ...06 B1
Bothwell St EH7 ....16 C2
Boundary Rd E EH14 .44 B4
Boundary Rd N EH14 .44 A3
Bowhill Terr EH3 ...15 A4
Bowling Gn, The EH6 .08 B1
Bowmont Pl EH8 ....65 B1
Boyd's Entry EH1 ...64 B3

Braefoot Terr 2
  EH9 ....38 C1
Braehead Ave EH4 ..10 C3
Braehead Bank EH4 .10 C3
Braehead Cres EH4 .10 C3
Braehead Dr EH4 ...10 C3
Braehead Gr EH4 ...10 C3
Braehead Loan EH4 .10 C3
Braehead Pk EH4 ...10 C3
Braehead Rd EH4 ...10 C3
Braehead Row EH4 .10 C3
Braehead View EH4 .10 C3
Braepark Rd EH4 ...10 C3
Brae Pk EH4 ....10 C4
Braid Ave EH10 .....37 A2
Braidburn Cres EH10 .36 C1
Braidburn Terr EH10 .36 C1
Braid Cres EH10 ....36 C1
Braid Farm Rd EH10 .37 A1
Braid Hills App EH10 .49 A4
Braid Hills Cres EH10 .48 C4
Braid Hills Dr
  EH10 ....37 B1
  EH16 ....49 C4
Braid Hills Rd EH10 .49 A4
Braid Mount EH10 ..49 A4
Braid Mount Crest
  EH10 ....49 A4
Braid Mount Rise
  EH10 ....49 A4
Braid Mount View
  EH10 ....49 A4
Braid Rd
  Edinburgh EH10 ....36 C1
  EH10 ....48 C4
Bramble Dr EH4 ....11 A2
Bramdean Gr EH10 .49 A4
Bramdean Pl EH10 .49 A4
Bramdean Rise EH10 .49 A4
Bramdean View
  EH10 ....49 A4
Brand Dr EH15 .....29 A2
Brandfield St EH3 ...63 A1
Brand Gdns EH15 ...29 B3
Brandon St EH3 ....15 B2
Brandon Terr EH3 ..15 B3
Breadalbane St
  Edinburgh EH6 ....08 A1
  EH6 ....16 A4
Breadalbane Terr
  EH11 ....63 A2
Bread St EH3 ....63 B2
Bread St La EH3 ....63 B2
Briarbank Terr EH11 .36 A4
Brickfield EH15 ....18 C1
Bridge End EH16 ...39 A3
Bridge Pl 4 EH3 ....14 C2
Bridge St
  Edinburgh EH15 ...18 C1
  Musselburgh EH21 .31 B2
Bridge St La EH11 ..18 C1
Briery Bauks EH8 ...65 B2
Brighton Pl EH15 ...28 C4
Brighton St EH1 ....65 A2
Bright's Cres EH9 ..38 B4
Bright Terr EH11 ...63 A2
Bristo Pl EH1 ......65 A2
Bristo Port EH1 ....65 A2
Bristo Sq EH1 ......65 A2
Britwell Cres EH7 ..17 C1
Broad Wynd EH6 ...08 C1
Broombank Terr
  EH12 ....33 C4
Broomburn Gr EH12 .34 A4
Broomfield Cres
  EH12 ....34 A4
Broomhall Ave EH12 .34 A4
Broomhall Bank
  EH12 ....21 C1
Broomhall Cres EH12 .21 C1
Broomhall Dr EH12 .21 B1
Broomhall Gdns
  EH12 ....21 C1
Broomhall Loan
  EH12 ....21 C1
Broomhall Pk EH12 .21 C1
Broomhall Pl EH12 .21 C1
Broomhall Rd EH12 .21 C1
Broomhall Terr EH12 .21 B1
Broomhouse Ave
  EH11 ....33 C3
Broomhouse Bank
  EH11 ....34 A3
Broomhouse Cotts
  EH11 ....33 C4
Broomhouse Cres
  EH11 ....34 A4
Broomhouse Ct EH11 .34 A3
Broomhouse Dr
  EH11 ....34 A4
Broomhouse Gdns E
  EH11 ....34 A4

Comely Bank Row *continued*
Comely Bank EH4 ....62 A4
Comely Bank St EH4 ..14 B2
Comely Bank Terr **1** EH4 ....14 C2
Comely Gn Cres **2** EH4 ....16 C1
Comiston Dr EH10 ....16 C1
Comiston Gdns EH10 ..36 B2
Comiston Pl EH10 ....48 C3
Comiston Pl EH10 ....37 A2
Comiston Prim Sch EH13 ....48 B2
Comiston Rd
  Edinburgh EH6 ......36 C1
  Comiston EH10 ......48 C3
Comiston Rise EH10 ..48 C3
Comiston Springs Ave EH10 ....48 C3
Comiston Terr EH10 ..36 C2
Comiston View EH10 ..48 C3
Commercial St EH6 ..08 B2
Conference Sq EH3 ..63 B2
Connaught Pl EH6 ....07 C1
Considine Gdns **3** EH8 ....17 B1
Considine Terr **2** EH8 ....17 B1
Constitution Pl EH6 ..08 C2
Constitution St
  Edinburgh EH6 ......08 C1
Cook's Cl EH8 ....16 B4
Cooper's Cl EH8 ......64 B3
Corbiehill Ave EH4 ..12 C3
Corbiehill Cres EH4 ..12 C3
Corbiehill Gdns EH4 ..12 C3
Corbiehill Gr EH4 ....12 B3
Corbiehill Pk EH4 ....12 B3
Corbiehill Pl EH4 ....12 B3
Corbiehill Rd EH4 ....12 B3
Corbiehill Terr EH4 ..12 B3
Corbieshot EH15 ....29 A1
Corbiewynd EH15 ....29 A1
Cordiner's Land EH1 ..63 C2
Cornhill Terr EH6 ....17 A4
Cornwallis Pl EH3 ....63 B3
Cornwall St EH1 ......63 B2
Corrennie Dr EH10 ..37 A2
Corrennie Gdns EH10 ....37 A1
Corslet Cres EH14 ..45 A1
Corslet Pl EH14 ......44 C1
Corslet Rd EH14 ....44 C1
Corstorphine Bank Ave EH12 ....21 B3
Corstorphine Bank Dr EH12 ....21 B3
Corstorphine Bank Terr EH12 ....21 B3
Corstorphine High St EH12 ....21 C2
Corstorphine Hill Ave EH12 ....22 A3
Corstorphine Hill Cres EH12 ....22 A3
Corstorphine Hill Gdns EH12 ....22 A3
Corstorphine Hill Rd EH12 ....22 A3
Corstorphine Ho Ave EH12 ....22 A2
Corstorphine Hopl
Corstorphine Pk Gdns EH12 ....22 A2
Corstorphine Prim Sch EH12 ....21 C1
Corstorphine Rd
  Edinburgh EH12 ......22 B2
  Edinburgh EH12 ......23 A3
Corunna Pl EH6 ......08 B1
Cottage Gn EH4 ......11 A4
Cottage Homes EH13 ..47 A2
Cottage Pk EH4 ......12 C1
Couperfield EH6 ......08 B2
Couper St EH6 ......08 B2
Coville Pl EH3 ......15 A2
Cowan Rd EH11 ......14 B4
Cowan's Cl EH8 ......65 B1
Cowgate
Cowgatehead EH1 ....65 A2
Cowpits Ford Rd EH21 ....43 B3
Cowpits Rd EH21 ....43 C2
Coxfield EH11 ....35 B4
Craigbrook Ave EH4 ....13 A1
Craigbrook Pl **6** EH4 ....13 B2
Craigbrook Terr **5** EH4 ....13 B2
Craigcrook Ave EH4 ..12 C2
Craigcrook Gr EH4 ..12 C1
Craigcrook Pk EH4 ..12 C1
Craigcrook Rd
  Edinburgh EH4 ......12 B2

Craigcrook Rd *continued*
  Edinburgh EH4 ......12 C1
Craigcrook Sq EH4 ..12 C2
Craigend Pk EH16 ..39 B1
Craigentinny Ave N EH7 ....18 A2
Craigentinny Ave EH6 ....17 C4
Craigentinny Cres EH7 ....18 A1
Craigentinny Gr EH7 ..18 A1
Craigentinny Prim Sch EH7 ....17 C2
Craigentinny Rd EH7 ..17 C2
Craighall Ave EH6 ....07 B2
Craighall Bank EH6 ..07 B2
Craighall Cres EH6 ..07 B2
Craighall Gdns EH6 ..07 B1
Craighall Rd EH6 ....07 B1
Craighall Terr EH6 ..07 B1
Craighouse Ave EH10 ..36 B2
Craighouse Gdns EH10 ....36 B2
Craighouse Pk EH10 ..36 B2
Craighouse Rd EH10 ..36 B2
Craighouse Terr EH10 ....36 B2
Craigievar Sq EH12 ..21 A4
Craigievar Wynd EH12 ....20 C3
Craiglea Dr EH10 ....36 C1
Craigleith Ave N
  9 Edinburgh EH4 ..13 B2
Craigleith Ave S EH4 ..23 B4
Craigleith Cres
  Edinburgh EH4 ......13 B1
Craigleith Dr EH4 ....13 C1
Craigleith Gdns EH4 ..13 C1
Craigleith Gr EH4 ....13 C1
Craigleith Hill Ave EH4 ....13 C2
Craigleith Hill Cres EH4 ....13 C2
Craigleith Hill Gdns EH4 ....13 C2
Craigleith Hill Gn EH4 ....13 C2
Craigleith Hill Gr EH4 ....13 C2
Craigleith Hill Loan EH4 ....13 C2
Craigleith Hill Pk EH4 ....13 C2
Craigleith Hill Row EH4 ....13 C2
Craigleith Ret Pk EH4 ..13 C1
Craigleith Rise EH4 ..23 B4
Craigleith View EH4 ..23 B4
Craigleith Hill Cres EH4 ....13 C2
Craiglockhart Ave EH14 ....35 B2
Craiglockhart Bank EH14 ....35 B1
Craiglockhart Cres EH14 ....35 B1
Craiglockhart Dell Rd EH14 ....35 B2
Craiglockhart Dr N EH14 ....35 B2
Craiglockhart Dr S
  Edinburgh EH14 ....35 B1
  Edinburgh EH14 ....47 A4
Craiglockhart Gdns EH14 ....35 B1
Craiglockhart Gr EH14 ....47 B4
Craiglockhart Loan EH14 ....35 B2
Craiglockhart Pk EH14 ....35 B1
Craiglockhart Pl EH14 ....35 B1
Craiglockhart Prim Sch EH11 ....36 A4
Craiglockhart Quadrant EH14 ....35 B1
Craiglockhart Rd
  Edinburgh EH14 ....35 B1
  Edinburgh EH14 ....47 A4
Craiglockhart Rd N EH14 ....35 C2
Craiglockhart Sports Ctr
Craiglockhart View EH14 ....35 C2

Craigmillar Castle Ave
  EH16 ....39 C3
  Edinburgh EH16 ....40 A4
Craigmillar Castle Gdns EH16 ....39 C3
Craigmillar Castle Gr EH16 ....39 C4
Craigmillar Castle Loan EH16 ....40 A4
Craigmillar Castle Rd EH16 ....39 C3
Craigmillar Castle Terr EH16 ....39 C3
Craigmillar Pk EH16 ..38 C3
Craigmillar Prim Sch EH16 ....40 A4
Craigmount App EH12 ....21 B3
Craigmount Ave EH12 ....21 B3
Craigmount Ave N
  Edinburgh EH12 ....21 B4
  Edinburgh EH4,EH12 ..11 A1
Craigmount Bank EH4 ....11 A1
Craigmount Bank W EH4 ....11 A1
Craigmount Brae
  Edinburgh EH12 ....11 A1
  Edinburgh EH12 ....21 A4
Craigmount Cres EH12 ....21 A3
Craigmount Ct EH4 ..11 A2
Craigmount Dr EH12 ..21 A4
Craigmount Gdns EH12 ....21 A3
Craigmount Gr EH12 ..21 A3
Craigmount Gr N EH12 ....21 A3
Craigmount Hill EH4 ..11 A1
Craigmount Loan EH12 ....21 A4
Craigmount Pk EH12 ..21 A3
Craigmount Pl EH12 ..21 A3
Craigmount Sec Sch EH12 ....21 A3
Craigmount Terr EH12 ....21 A3
Craigmount View EH12 ....21 A4
Craigmount Way EH12 ....21 A4
Craigmuir Prim Sch EH4 ....5 B1
Craigour Ave EH17 ..51 C4
Craigour Cres EH17 ..52 A4
Craigour Dr EH17 ....52 A4
Craigour Gdns EH17 ..52 A4
Craigour Gn EH17 ....52 A4
Craigour Gr EH17 ....52 A4
Craigour Loan EH17 ..52 A4
Craigour Pl EH17 ....51 C4
Craigour Terr EH17 ..52 A4
Craigroyston Com High Sch EH4 ....13 A4
Craigroyston Gr EH4 ..12 C4
Craigroyston Pl EH4 ..04 C1
Craigs Ave
  Edinburgh EH12 ....21 A2
Craigs Bank EH12 ....21 A3
Craigs Cres EH12 ....21 B3
Craigs Dr EH12 ......21 A3
Craigs Gdns EH12 ....21 A3
Craigs Gr EH12 ......21 B3
Craigs Loan EH12 ....21 B3
Craigs Pk EH12 ......21 A3
Craigs Rd EH12 ......20 C3
Cramond Ave EH4 ....03 A1
Cramond Bridge Cottages EH4 ....10 B4
Cramond Brig Toll EH4 ....10 B4
Cramond Cres EH4 ..03 A1
Cramond Gdns EH4 ..03 A1
Cramond Glebe Gdns EH4 ....03 A2
Cramond Glebe Rd EH4 ....03 A2
Cramond Glebe Terr EH4 ....03 A2
Cramond Gn EH4 ....03 A2
Cramond Pk EH4 ....03 A1
Cramond Pl EH4 ....03 A1
Cramond Prim Sch EH4 ....3 A2
Cramond Rd N EH4 ..03 B2
Cramond Rd S EH4 ..04 A1
Cramond Regis EH4 ..11 A4
Cramond Roman Fort* EH4 ....03 A3
Cramond Terr EH4 ..03 A1
Cramond Vale EH4 ..02 C1
Cramond Village EH4 ....03 A2
Cranston St EH8 ....64 B3

Crarae Ave EH4 ......23 C4
Craufurdland EH4 ....10 C3
Crawfurd Rd EH16 ..38 B3
Cres,The EH10 ......36 C2
Crewe Bank EH5 ....06 A1
Crewe Cres EH5 ....06 A1
Crewe Gr EH5 ......06 A1
Crewe Loan EH5 ....05 C1
Crewe Pl EH5 ......05 C1
Crewe Rd Gdns EH5 ..05 C1
Crewe Rd N EH5 ....05 C1
Crewe Rd S EH4 ....14 A3
Crewe Rd W EH5 ....05 C1
Crewe Terr EH5 ....06 A1
Crichton St EH8 ....65 A2
Crighton Pl **3** EH7 ..16 B3
Croft-An-Righ EH8 ..64 C4
Cromwell Pl EH6 ....08 B2
Crown Pl EH6 ......08 A2
Crown St EH6 ......08 A2
Cuddies La EH13 ....47 A3
Cuddy La EH10 ......36 C2
Cuguen Pl EH18 ....61 A1
Cultins Rd EH11 ....33 A3
Cumberland St EH3 ..15 B2
Cumin Pl EH9 ......26 A1
Cumlodden Ave EH12 ....23 B4
Cumnor Cres
  Edinburgh EH16 ....38 C3
  Edinburgh EH16 ....39 A1
Curriehill Rd EH14 ..44 B1
Curriehill Sta EH14 ..44 B1

D

Daiches Braes EH15 ..29 C2
Daisy Terr EH11 ....36 A4
Dalgety Ave EH7 ....17 A2
Dalgety Rd EH7 ....17 A2
Dalgety St EH7 ....17 A2
Dalhousie Terr EH10 ..36 B1
Dalkeith Ctry Pk* EH22 ....54 C2
Dalkeith Rd
  Edinburgh EH16 ....38 C4
  Edinburgh EH16 ....65 C1
Dalkeith St EH15 ....29 B3
Dalmeny Rd EH4 ....07 A1
Dalmeny St EH6 ....16 B3
Dalrymple Cres
  Edinburgh EH9 ....26 A1
  Musselburgh EH21 ..30 C3
Dalrymple Loan EH21 ....31 B2
Dalry Pl EH11 ......63 A2
Dairy Prim Sch EH11 ..24 B2
Dalry Rd
  Edinburgh EH11 ....24 B3
  Edinburgh EH11 ....63 A1
Dalziel Pl EH7 ......17 A1
Damside
  Edinburgh EH4 ....24 B4
  Edinburgh EH4 ....62 A3
Danderhall Cres EH22 ....53 A4
Dania Ct EH4 ......34 B4
Danube St EH4 ....62 A4
Darnaway St EH3 ..62 A4
Darnell Rd EH5 ....06 C1
Darroch Ct EH8 ....64 B3
Davidson Gdns EH4 ..12 C3
Davidson Pk EH4 ..14 A2
Davidson Rd EH4 ..13 C3
Davidson's Mains Prim Sch EH4 ....12 B3
Davies Row EH12 ..21 C2
Davie St EH8 ......65 B2
Dean Bank La EH3 ..15 A2
Deanery Cl EH7 ....17 B1
Dean Gallery* EH4 ..62 A3
Deanhaugh St EH4 ..15 A2
Dean Path
  Edinburgh EH4 ....14 B1
  Edinburgh EH4 ....62 A3
Dean Pk Cres EH4 ..62 A4
Dean Pk Mews EH4 ....14 C2
Dean Pk St EH4 ....14 C2
Dean St EH4 ......14 C2
Dean Terr EH4 ....62 B4
Dechmont Rd EH12 ..20 C3
Dell Rd EH13 ......47 A3
Delta Pl EH21 ......43 A4
Denham Gn Ave EH5 ..07 A1
Denham Gn Pl EH5 ..07 A1
Denham Gn Terr EH5 ....07 A1
Denholm Ave
  Musselburgh EH21 ..42 B4
  Musselburgh EH21 ..42 C4
Denholm Dr EH21 ..42 C4

Denholm Rd EH21 ..30 B1
Denholm Way EH21 ..42 B4
Derby St EH6 ......07 C2
Devon Pl EH12 ....24 B3
Dewar Pl EH3 ......63 A2
Dewar Pl La EH3 ..63 A2
Dick Pl EH9 ....37 C4
Dicksonfield EH7 ..16 A2
Dickson St EH6 ....16 B3
Dinmont Dr EH16 ..39 A2
Distillery La
  Edinburgh EH11 ..24 B3
  Edinburgh EH11 ..63 A2
Dochart Dr EH4 ....11 B1
Dock Pl EH6 ......08 B2
Dock St EH6 ......08 B2
Donaldson's Sch for the Deaf
  Edinburgh, Coates EH12 ....24 A3
  Edinburgh, Stockbridge EH4 ....15 A2
Dorset Pl
  Edinburgh EH11 ..24 C1
  Edinburgh EH11 ..63 A1
Double Dykes EH21 ..43 C4
Double Hedges Pk EH16 ....38 C1
Double Hedges Rd EH16 ....38 C1
Douglas Cres EH12 ..24 B4
Douglas Gdns EH4 ..24 B4
Douglas Gdns Mews EH4 ....24 B4
Douglas Terr EH11 ..63 A2
Doune Terr EH3 ....62 B4
Dovecot Gr EH14 ..34 C1
Dovecot Loan
  Edinburgh EH14 ....34 C1
Dovecot Pk EH14 ..46 C4
Dovecot Rd EH12 ..21 C1
Dowie's Mill Cottages EH4 ....10 B4
Dowie's Mill La EH4 ..10 B4
Downfield Pl EH11 ..24 B3
Downie Pl EH21 ....22 B2
Downie Pl EH21 ....31 B2
Downie Terr EH12 ..22 B2
Dreghorn Ave EH13 ..48 A1
Dreghorn Dr EH13 ..48 A1
Dreghorn Gdns EH13 ..48 A1
Dreghorn Junc EH13 ....48 A1
Dreghorn Link EH13 ..48 A1
Dreghorn Loan EH13 ..47 A2
Dreghorn Pk EH13 ..47 C2
Dreghorn Pl EH13 ..48 A1
Drum Ave EH17 ....52 A2
Drum Brae Ave EH12 ..21 B4
Drum Brae Cres EH4 ..11 B1
Drum Brae Dr EH4 ..11 C1
Drum Brae Gdns EH12 ....21 B4
Drum Brae La EH12 ..21 B4
Drum Brae N
  Edinburgh EH4 ....11 A2
  Edinburgh EH12 ..21 B4
Drum Brae Neuk EH12 ....21 B4
Drum Brae Pk EH12 ..21 B4
Drum Brae Pk App EH12 ....21 B4
Drum Brae Pl EH12 ..21 B4
Drum Brae Prim Sch EH4 ....21 A4
Drum Brae S
  Edinburgh EH12 ..11 B1
  Edinburgh EH12 ..21 B4
Drum Brae Wlk EH4 ..11 A1
Drum Cotts EH17 ..52 B1
Drum Pl EH17 ......52 B1
Drum St EH17 ......52 B2
Drum View Ave EH22 ..53 A3
Dryden Gait EH7 ..16 A3
Dryden Gdns EH7 ..16 A3
Dryden Pl EH9 ......26 B1
Dryden St EH7 ....16 A3
Dryden Terr EH7 ..16 A3
Drylaw Ave EH4 ....13 B2
Drylaw Cres EH4 ....13 A3
Drylaw Gdns EH4 ..13 A3
Drylaw Gn EH4 ....13 A3
Drylaw Ho Gdns EH4 ..13 A3

Drylaw Ho Paddock EH4 ....13 A3
Drylaw Specl Sch EH4 ....13 B3
Duart Cres EH4 ....11 B1
Dublin Meuse **1** 15 B1
Dublin St
  Edinburgh EH1 ....15 C2
  Edinburgh EH3 ....64 A4
Dublin St La N **3** EH1 ....15 C2
Dublin St La S EH1 ..64 A4
Duddingston Ave EH15 ....28 A2
Duddingston Cres EH15 ....28 C2
Duddingston Gdns S EH15 ....28 B3
Duddingston Gr E EH15 ....28 B3
Duddingston Gr W EH15 ....28 B2
Duddingston Loan EH15 ....28 A2
Duddingston Mains Cotts EH15 ....29 A2
Duddingston Mills EH8 ....28 A3
Duddingston Pk EH15 ....28 C3
Duddingston Pk S EH15 ....28 C1
Duddingston Prim Sch EH15 ....28 A3
Duddingston Rd EH15 ....28 B3
Duddingston Rd W EH15 ....27 C1
Duddingston Rise EH15 ....28 B2
Duddingston Row EH15 ....28 B2
Duddingston Sq E EH15 ....28 B3
Duddingston Sq W EH15 ....28 B3
Duddingston View EH15 ....28 B2
Duddingston Yds EH15 ....28 B2
Duddingston Gdns N EH15 ....28 B3
Dudley Ave EH6 ....07 C2
Dudley Ave S EH6 ..07 C2
Dudley Bank EH6 ..07 C2
Dudley Cres EH6 ..07 C2
Dudley Gdns EH6 ..07 C2
Dudley Gr EH6 ....07 C2
Dudley Terr EH6 ..07 C2
Duff Rd EH11 ......24 B2
Duff St EH11 ......24 B2
Duff St La EH11 ....24 A2
Duke Pl EH6 ......16 C4
Duke St EH6 ......16 C4
Duke's Wlk EH8 ....45 C4
Dumbeg Pk EH14 ..45 C4
Dumbiedykes Rd EH8 ....65 C3
Dumbryden Dr EH14 ..34 B1
Dumbryden Gdns EH14 ....34 B2
Dumbryden Gr EH14 ..34 A1
Dumbryden Ind Est EH14 ....34 B1
Dumbryden Rd EH14 ..34 B1
Dunard Gdn EH9 ..37 C3
Dunbar St EH3 ....63 B2
Duncan Pl EH6 ....16 C4
Dundas St
  Edinburgh EH3 ....15 B2
  Edinburgh EH3 ....62 C4
Dundee St
  Edinburgh EH11 ..24 B2
  Edinburgh EH11 ..63 A1
Dundee Terr EH11 ..24 B1
Dundonald St EH3 ..15 B2
Dunedin St EH7 ....15 C3
Dunlop Ct EH12 ....15 C3
Dunollie Ct EH12 ..21 A3
Dunrobin Pl EH3 ..15 A2
Dunsmuir Ct EH12 ..21 C1
Dunvegan Ct EH4 ..11 A4
Durar Dr EH4 ......11 B1
Durham Ave EH15 ..28 B3
Durham Dr EH15 ..28 C2
Durham Gdns N EH15 ....28 C3
Durham Gdns S EH15 ....28 C3
Durham Pl E EH15 ..28 C3
Durham Pl La EH15 ..28 C3

Durham PI W EH15 .....28 B2
Durham Rd EH15 ....25 C2
Durham Sq EH15 ....28 C2
Durham Sq
  Edinburgh EH15 ....28 B3
  Edinburgh EH15 ....28 C3
Durham Terr EH15 .....28 C3
Durwood Gr EH16 .....39 A2

E

Eagle Rock★ EH4 ....2 C3
Earl Grey St EH3 ......63 B2
Earl Haig Gdns EH5 ....07 A1
Earlston PI 6 EH7 ......16 C1
East Adam St EH8 ......65 B2
East Barnton Ave
  EH4 ....12 A3
East Barnton Gdns
  EH4 ....12 A3
East Brighton Cres
  EH15 ....28 C4
East Caystane PI
  EH10 ....48 C2
East Camus PI EH10 ...48 C2
East Camus Rd EH10 ..48 C2
East Castle Rd EH10 ..24 C1
East Champanyie
  EH9 ....38 A2
East Clapperfield
  EH16 ....38 C1
East Claremont St
  EH7 ....15 C2
East Comiston EH10 ...48 C2
East Craigs Prim Sch
  EH12 ....21 A4
East Craigs Rigg
  EH12 ....21 A4
East Cromwell St
  EH6 ....08 B2
East Crosscauseway
  EH8 ....65 B1
East Ct
  Edinburgh, Greendykes
  8 ....40 A3
  8 Edinburgh, Ravelston
  EH4 ....13 B2
Easter Belmont Rd
  EH12 ....23 A3
Easter Currie Cres
  EH14 ....44 C1
Easter Currie PI
  EH14 ....44 C1
Easter Dairy Dr 3
  EH11 ....24 B2
Easter Dairy PI 1
  EH11 ....24 B2
Easter Dairy Rd EH11 ..24 B2
Easter Dairy Rigg 2
  EH11 ....24 B2
Easter Dairy Wynd
  EH11 ....24 B2
Easter Drylaw Ave
  EH4 ....13 B3
Easter Drylaw Bank
  EH4 ....13 B4
Easter Drylaw Dr
  EH4 ....13 C3
Easter Drylaw Gdns
  EH4 ....13 B3
Easter Drylaw Gr
  EH4 ....13 B3
Easter Drylaw Loan
  EH4 ....13 B3
Easter Drylaw PI EH4 ..13 B4
Easter Drylaw View
  EH4 ....13 B4
Easter Drylaw Way
  EH4 ....13 B3
Easter Haugh EH13 ....48 A3
Easter Hermitage
  EH6 ....17 A3
Eastern General Hospl
  EH6 ....17 C3
Eastern Ind Est EH15 ..41 B4
Easter Pk Dr EH4 ......12 A4
Easter Rd
  Edinburgh EH7 ....16 B2
  Edinburgh EH7 ....64 C4
Easter Rd Stad
  (Hibernian FC) EH7 ...16 C2
Easter Steil EH10 ......36 B1
Easter Warriston
  EH7 ....15 B4
East Farm Of Gilmerton
  EH17 ....52 B2
East Fettes Ave EH4 ...14 B3
Eastfield EH15 ....30 B3
Eastfield Gdns EH15 ...30 A3
Eastfield PI EH15 ......30 B3
East Fountainbridge
  EH3 ....63 B2
East Hermitage PI
  EH6 ....16 C4

East Kilngate PI
  EH17 ....51 C1
East Kilngate Rigg
  EH17 ....51 C1
East Kilngate Wynd
  EH17 ....51 C1
East Lillypot EH5 ......07 A1
East London St EH7 ....15 C2
East Mayfield EH9 .....38 B4
East Mkt St EH8 ....64 B3
East Montgomery PI 4
  EH7 ....16 B2
East Newington PI
  EH9 ....26 B1
East Norton PI 9
  EH7 ....16 B2
East Parkside EH16 ....65 C1
East Preston St
  Edinburgh EH8 ....26 A1
  Edinburgh EH8 ....65 C1
East Preston St La 8
  EH8 ....26 A1
East Restairig Terr
  EH6 ....17 A4
East Savile Rd EH16 ...38 B3
East Sciennes St 2
  EH9 ....26 A1
East Scotland St La 2
  EH3 ....15 C2
East Silvermills La
  EH3 ....15 A2
East Suffolk Rd EH16 ..38 C3
East Telferton EH7 .....17 A3
East Trinity Rd EH5 ....07 A2
East Werberside EH4 ..14 A4
East Werberside PI
  EH4 ....14 A4
Eden La EH10 ....37 A3
Edgefield Ind Est
  EH20 ....59 B1
Edgefield Rd EH20 .....59 B1
Edina PI EH7 ....16 C2
Edina St EH7 ....16 C2
Edinburgh Acad (Prep
  Sch) The EH3 ....14 C4
Edinburgh Acad
  (UpperSch) EH3 ......15 A2
Edinburgh Butterfly &
  Insect World★
  EH18 ....61 B3
Edinburgh Castle★
  EH1 ....62 C3
Edinburgh Coll of Art
  EH3 ....63 C2
Edinburgh Fort Ret Pk
  EH15 ....21 A1
Edinburgh Pk
  Edinburgh EH12 ......20 B1
  Edinburgh EH12 ......32 C4
Edinburgh Rd EH21 ....30 C2
Edinburgh West Off Pk
  EH12 ....32 C4
Edinburgh Zoo (Royal
  Zoological Society of
  Scotland)★ EH12 ...22 B3
Edmonstone Ave
  EH22 ....53 A4
Edmonstone Dr EH22 ..53 A3
Edmonstone Rd
  Danderhall EH22 .....53 A4
  Danderhall EH22 .....53 A4
Edmonstone Terr
  EH22 ....53 A4
Eglinton Cres EH12 ....24 B3
Egypt Mews EH9 ....37 B3
Eildon St EH3 ....15 B3
Eildon Terr EH3 ....15 A4
Elbe St EH6 ....08 C1
Elcho Terr EH15 ....29 B4
Elder St EH1 ....64 A4
Elder St E EH1 ....64 A4
Eldin Ind Est EH20 .....59 B2
Eldin PI EH18 ....60 C1
Electra PI EH15 ....08 B2
Elgin St EH7 ....16 B2
Elgin St N EH7 ....16 B2
Elgin Terr EH7 ....16 B2
Elizafield EH6 ....16 A4
Ellangowan Terr
  EH16 ....39 A1
Ellen's Glen Loan
  EH17 ....51 B2
Ellen's Glen Rd EH16,
  EH17 ....51 B2
Ellersly Rd EH12 ....23 B3
Elliot Gdns EH14 ....47 A4
Elliot PI EH14 ....47 A4
Elliot Pk EH14 ....47 A4
Elliot Rd EH14 ....47 A4
Elliot St EH7 ....16 C2
Elm PI EH6 ....16 C4
Elm Row
  Bonnyrigg and Lasswade
  EH18 ....60 C1
  Edinburgh EH7 ....16 B2
Elmwood Tr EH6 ....17 A4
Eltringham Gdns
  EH14 ....35 B4

Eltringham Gr EH14 ...35 B4
Eltringham Terr
  EH14 ....35 B4
Esdaile Bank EH9 ......37 C4
Esdaile PI EH9 ....37 C4
Eskbank Rd Rdbt
  EH22 ....61 C1
Eskdale Mews EH21 ...31 B2
Eskfield Gr EH22 ....61 C2
Eskside E EH21 ....31 B2
Eskside W EH21 ....31 B2
Eskview Ave EH21 .....31 A1
Eskview Cres EH21 ....31 A1
Eskview Gr EH21 ......31 A1
Eskview Rd EH21 ......31 A1
Eskview Terr EH21 .....31 A1
Esplanade Terr EH15 ..29 C4
Essendean PI EH14 ....11 C1
Essendean Terr EH14 ..11 C1
Essex Brae EH4 ....10 C4
Essex Pk EH4 ....10 C4
Essex Rd EH4 ....10 C4
Esslemont Rd EH16 ....38 B2
Ethel Terr EH10 ....36 C2
Eton Terr EH4 ....62 A4
Ettrickdale PI EH3 .....15 A3
Ettrick Gr EH10 ....24 C1
Ettrick Loan EH10 .....36 B4
Ettrick Rd EH10 ....36 B4
Eva PI EH9 ....38 A2
Ewerland EH4 ....10 C4
Eyre Cres EH3 ....15 B2
Eyre PI EH3 ....15 B2
Eyre Terr EH3 ....15 B2**

F

Fair-a-far EH4 ....03 A1
Fair-a-far Cotts EH4 ..03 A1
Fair-a-far Shot EH4 ...03 A1
Fairbrae EH11 ....34 B3
Fairford Gdns EH16 ....39 A1
Fairmile Ave EH10 .....49 A2
Faith Mission Coll The
  EH17 ....52 A2
Falcon Ave EH10 ......37 A3
Falcon Ct EH10 ....37 A3
Falcon Gdns EH10 ....37 A3
Falcon Rd EH10 ....37 A3
Falcon Rd W EH10 ....37 A3
Falkland Gdns EH12 ...12 A1
Farrer Gr EH7 ....18 A1
Farrer Terr EH7 ....18 A1
Farteviot Royal Hospl for
  Sick Children EH9 ...37 B4
Fauldburn EH12 ....11 A1
Fauldburn Pk EH12 ...11 A1
Featherhall Ave
  EH12 ....21 C2
Featherhall Cres N
  EH12 ....21 B2
Featherhall Cres S
  EH12 ....21 B2
Featherhall Gr EH12 ..21 C2
Featherhall PI EH12 ...21 C2
Featherhall Terr
  EH12 ....21 C2
Ferguson Ct EH21 .....43 B3
Ferguson Dr EH21 .....43 A3
Ferguson Gdns EH21 ..43 B3
Ferguson Gn EH21 ....43 A3
Ferguson View EH21 ..43 A3
Ferniehill Ave EH17 ...52 A2
Ferniehill Dr EH17 ....52 A2
Ferniehill Gdns EH17 ..52 B3
Ferniehill PI EH17 .....52 A2
Ferniehill Rd EH17 ....52 A2
Ferniehill Sq EH17 ....52 A2
Ferniehill St EH17 .....52 A3
Ferniehill Terr EH17 ...52 A2
Ferniehill Way EH17 ...52 A2
Fernielaw Ave EH13 ...46 C1
Fernieside Ave EH17 ..52 A3
Fernieside Cres
  EH17 ....52 A3
Fernieside Dr EH17 ...52 A4
Fernieside Gdns
  EH17 ....52 A3
Fernieside Gr EH17 ...52 B3
Fernieside Prim Sch
  EH17 ....52 A3
Ferryfield EH5 ....06 B1
Ferryhill Prim Sch
  EH4 ....13 B3
Ferry Rd
  Edinburgh, EH5 ....13 A4
  Edinburgh EH5 ....07 B1
Ferry Rd Ave EH4 .....13 B4
Ferry Rd Dr EH4 ......05 C1
Ferry Rd Gdns EH4 ...13 A4
Ferry Rd Gr EH4 ......13 B4
Ferry Rd PI EH4 ....13 B4
Festival Sq EH3 ....63 B2
Fettes Ave EH4 ....14 B2
Fettes Coll EH4 ....14 B3
Fettes Rise EH4 ....14 B4

Fettes Row EH3 ....15 B2
Figgate Bank EH15 ....19 A1
Figgate La EH15 ......19 A1
Figgate St EH15 ......19 A1
Fillyside Ave EH7 .....18 A2
Fillyside Rd EH7 ......18 A3
Fillyside Terr EH7 .....18 A3
Findlay Ave EH7 ......17 B3
Findlay Cotts EH7 .....17 B3
Findlay Gdns EH7 .....17 B3
Findlay Gr EH7 ....17 B3
Findlay Medway EH7 ..17 B3
Fingal PI EH9 ....65 A1
Fishers Wynd EH21 ...31 A2
Fishmarket Sq EH6 ....07 C3
Fishwives' Cswy
  Edinburgh EH1 ....18 C1
  Edinburgh EH7, EH15 .18 B1
Fleshmarket Cl EH1 ...64 A3
Flora Stevenson Prim Sch
  EH4 ....14 B2
Forbes Rd EH10 ....37 A4
Forbes St EH8 ....65 B1
Ford's Rd EH11 ....35 A4
Forres St EH3 ....62 B4
Forrester High Sch
  EH12 ....33 C4
Forrester Pk Ave
  EH12 ....33 C4
Forrester Pk Dr
  EH12 ....33 C4
Forrester Pk Gdns
  EH12 ....33 C4
Forrester Pk Gn
  EH12 ....34 A4
Forrester Pk Gr EH12 ..33 C4
Forrester Pk Loan
  EH12 ....33 C4
Forrester Pk Rd
  EH12 ....33 C4
Forrester Rd EH12 ....21 C3
Forrest Hill EH1 ......65 A2
Forrest Rd EH1 ....65 A2
Forth Ind Est EH5 .....6 A3
Forth Ho EH6 ....08 A2
Forth St EH1 ....15 C1
Forth View Cres
  Currie EH14 ....44 B1
  Danderhall EH22 .....53 A4
Forthview Rd EH4 .....13 B2
Forthview Terr EH14 ..13 A2
Foulis Cres EH14 ......45 C2
Foundry La EH20 .....59 C1
Fountainbridge EH3 ...63 A1
Fountainhall Rd EH9 ...38 A4
Fourth Gait EH14 .....44 A3
Fowler Terr EH11 .....24 B1
Fox Covert Ave EH12 ..12 A1
Fox Covert RC Prim Schs
  EH12 ....12 A1
Fox Spring Cres
  EH10 ....48 C3
Fox Spring Rise
  EH10 ....48 C3
Fox St EH6 ....09 A1
Fraser Ave EH5 ....06 C1
Fraser Cres EH5 ......06 C1
Fraser Gdns EH5 .....06 C1
Fraser Gr EH5 ....06 C1
Frederick St EH2 ......62 C4
Frogston Ave EH10 ...49 A1
Frogston Brae EH17 ..58 A4
Frogston Gdns EH10 ..49 A1
Frogston Gr EH10 ....49 A1
Frogston Rd E EH17 ..50 B1
Frogston Rd W EH10 ..57 B4
Frogston Terr EH10 ...49 B1
Furcheons Pk EH8 ....28 A4

G

Galachlawshot EH10 ..49 B2
Galachlawside EH10 ..49 B1
Galloee, The EH13 ....47 C2
Gamekeeper's Loan
  EH4 ....03 A1
Gamekeeper's Pk
  EH4 ....03 A1
Gamekeeper's Rd
  EH4 ....03 A1
Garden Terr EH4 ......12 A4
Gardiner Gr EH4 ......13 A2
Gardiner Rd \011
  EH4 ....13 A2
Gardiner Terr EH4 ....13 A1

Gardner's Cres EH3 ...63 B2
Garscube Terr EH12 ...23 C4
Gayfield Cl 8 EH1 .....16 A2
Gayfield PI La EH1 ....16 A2
Gayfield Sq
  Edinburgh EH1 ....15 C2
  Edinburgh EH1 ....16 A2
Gayfield St EH1 ....15 C2
Gayfield St La 7
  EH1 ....15 C2
Gelnorchy Terr EH9 ...38 B4
Gentiles Entry EH8 ....64 C3
George Heriot's Sch
  EH1 ....65 A2
George IV Bridge 64 A2
George Sq EH8 ....65 A1
George Sq La EH8 ....65 A1
George St EH2 ....62 C3
George Watson's Coll
  EH10 ....36 C3
George Watson's Sch
  Lower Prim Sch
  EH10 ....36 B3
George Watson's Coll
  Upper Prim Sch
  EH10 ....36 B3
Georgian Ho★ EH2 ...62 B3
Gibbs Entry EH8 ......65 B2
Gibson St EH4 ....16 A4
Gibson Terr EH11 .....63 A1
Gifford Pk EH8 ....65 B1
Gilbersoun EH15 .....29 C1
Gilberstoun Brig
  EH15 ....29 C1
Gilbersoun Loan
  EH15 ....29 C1
Gilbertstoun PI EH15 ..29 C1
Gilbersoun Wynd
  EH15 ....29 C1
Giles St EH6 ....08 B1
Gillespie Cres EH10 ...63 B1
Gillespie PI EH10 .....63 B1
Gillespie Rd EH13 .....46 B2
Gillespie St EH3 ......63 B1
Gillsland Rd EH10 ....36 B4
Gilmerton Dykes Ave
  EH17 ....51 C1
Gilmerton Dykes Cres
  EH17 ....51 B2
Gilmerton Dykes Dr
  EH17 ....51 C1
Gilmerton Dykes Gr
  EH17 ....51 B2
Gilmerton Dykes Loan
  EH17 ....51 B1
Gilmerton Dykes PI
  EH17 ....51 B2
Gilmerton Dykes Rd
  Edinburgh EH17 ......51 C1
  Edinburgh EH17 ......59 C1
Gilmerton Dykes St
  EH17 ....51 C1
Gilmerton Dykes Terr
  EH17 ....51 C1
Gilmerton Dykes View
  EH17 ....51 C1
Gilmerton PI EH17 ...51 C1
Gilmerton Prim Sch
  EH17 ....51 C3
Gilmerton Rd
  Edinburgh EH16 ......39 A1
  Edinburgh EH17 ......51 C3
Gilmerton Rd Rdbt
  EH22 ....61 A1
Gilmerton Sta Rd
  EH17 ....60 A4
Gilmore PI EH11 ......63 A1
Gilmore PI EH3 ....63 A1
Gilmour PI La EH3 ....63 A1
Gilmour Rd EH16 .....38 B3
Gilmour St EH8 ......65 B2
Gladstone PI EH6 .....17 A4
Gladstone Terr EH9 ...26 A1
Glasgow Rd EH12 ....21 A2
Glebe Dr EH22 ....22 A2
Glebe Gdns EH12 ....21 C2
Glebe PI EH18 ....60 B1
Glebe Terr EH12 .....21 C2
Glebe, The EH4 ......03 A2
Glenallan Dr EH16 ...39 A2
Glenallan Loan EH16 ..39 A2
Glencairn Cres EH12 ..24 B3
Glendevon Ave EH12 ..23 A2
Glendevon Gdns
  EH12 ....23 A2
Glendevon Gr EH12 ...23 A2
Glendevon Pk EH12 ...23 A2
Glendevon PI EH12 ...23 A2
Glendevon Rd EH12 ...23 A2
Glendevon Terr EH12 ..23 A2
Glendinning Cres
  EH16 ....51 A4
Glenfinlas St EH3 .....62 B3
Glengyle Terr EH3 ....63 B1
Glenisla Gdns EH9 ....37 C3
Glenisla Gdns La
  EH9 ....37 C3

Glenlee Ave EH8 27
Glenlee Gdns EH8 27
Glenlockhart Bank
  EH14 35
Glenlockhart Rd
  EH14 36
Glenlockhart Valley
  EH14 35
Glenogle Ct EH3 15
Glenogle Ho 7 EH3 ...15
Glenogle PI 8 EH3 ...15
Glenogle Rd EH3 15
Glenogle Terr EH3 ...15
Glen St EH3 63
Glenure Loan EH4 ...11
Glenvarloch Cres
  EH16 51
  8 Edinburgh EH16 ...51
Gloucester La EH3 ...62
Gloucester PI EH3 ...62
Gloucester Sq EH3 ...62
Gloucester St EH3 ...62
Goff Ave EH7 18
Gogarloch Bank
  EH12 21
Gogarloch Haugh
  EH12 21
Gogarloch Muir
  EH12 21
Gogarloch Rd EH12 ..20
Gogarloch Syke
  EH12 20
Gogar Rdbt EH12 20
Gogar Sta Rd EH12 ..32
Goldenacre Terr EH3 ..15
Goose Gn Ave EH21 ..31
Goose Gn Cres EH21 ..31
Goose Gn PI EH21 ...31
Goose Gn Rd EH21 ...31
Gordon Loan EH12 ...22
Gordon Rd EH12 22
Gordon St EH6 16
Gordon Terr EH16 ...38
Gorgie PK Cl EH14 ...35
Gorgie Pk Rd
  Edinburgh EH11 23
  Edinburgh EH14 35
Gorgie Rd EH11 35
Gosford PI EH6 07
Gracefield Ct EH21 ...31
Gracemount Ave
  EH16 51
Gracemount Bsns Pav
  EH16 51
Gracemount Dr EH16 ..51
Gracemount High Sch
  EH16 51
Gracemount PI EH16 ..51
Gracemount Prim Sch
  EH16 51
Gracemount Rd
  EH16 50
Gracemount Sq EH16 ..51
Graham St EH6 08
Granby Rd EH16 38
Grandfield EH6 07
Grandville EH6 07
Grange Cres EH9 37
Grange Ct EH9 26
Grange Loan EH9 37
Grange Loan Gdns
  EH9 37
Grange Rd EH9 25
Grange Terr EH9 37
Grannus Mews EH21 ..31
Grant Ave EH13 46
Granton Cres EH5 ...06
Granton Gr EH5 06
Granton Gr EH5 06
Granton Mains Ave
  EH4 05
Granton Mains Bank
  EH4 05
Granton Mains Brae
  EH4 05
Granton Mains Ct
  EH4 05
Granton Mains E EH4 ..05
Granton Mains Gate
  EH4 05
Granton Mains Vale
  EH4 05
Granton Mains Wynd
  EH4 05
Granton Medway
  EH5 06
Granton Mill Cres
  EH4 05
Granton Mill Dr EH4 ..05
Granton Mill March
  EH4 05
Granton Mill Pk EH4 ..05
Granton Mill PI EH4 ..05
Granton Mill W EH4 ..05
Granton Pk Ave EH5 ..06
Granton PI EH5 06
Granton Prim Sch EH5 ..6

Granton Rd
Edinburgh EH5 ......06 B3
Edinburgh EH5 ......06 C2
Granton Sq EH5 ......06 B3
Granton Terr EH5 ......06 B2
Granton View EH5 ......06 B2
Grantully Pl EH9 ......38 B4
Granville Terr EH11 ......24 C1
Grassmarket EH1 ......63 C2
Gray's Ct EH8 ......65 B2
Gray's Loan EH11,
EH10 ......36 A4
Graysmill Specl Sch
EH14 ......35 B1
Great Cannon Bank
EH15 ......18 C1
Great Carleton Pl
EH16 ......40 C3
Great Carleton Sq
EH16 ......40 C3
Great Junc St EH6 ......08 B1
Great King St EH3 ......15 B2
Great Michael Cl
EH6 ......07 C3
Great Michael Rise
EH6 ......07 C2
Great Michael Sq
EH6 ......07 C3
Great Stuart St
Edinburgh EH3 ......62 A3
Edinburgh EH3 ......62 B4
Greenacre EH14 ......46 A4
Greenbank Ave EH10 ......36 C1
Greenbank Cres
Edinburgh EH10 ......36 C1
Edinburgh EH10 ......48 B3
Greenbank Dr
Edinburgh EH10 ......36 B1
Edinburgh EH10 ......48 A4
Greenbank Gdns
EH10 ......48 B4
Greenbank Gr EH10 ......48 B4
Greenbank La EH10 ......36 B1
Greenbank Loan
EH10 ......36 B1
Greenbank Pk EH10 ......36 C1
Greenbank Rd
Edinburgh EH10 ......36 B1
Edinburgh EH10 ......48 B4
Greenbank Rise
EH10 ......48 B3
Greenbank Row
EH10 ......48 B4
Greenbank Terr EH10 ......36 C1
Greendale Pk
Edinburgh EH4 ......12 C4
Edinburgh EH4 ......13 A4
Greendykes Ave
EH16 ......40 B3
Greendykes Dr EH16 ......40 B3
Greendykes Gdns
EH16 ......40 B3
Greendykes Loan 8
EH16 ......40 B3
Greendykes Prim Sch
EH16 ......40 B2
Greendykes Rd EH16 ......40 B2
Greendykes Terr
EH16 ......40 B3
Greenend Dr EH17 ......51 B4
Greenend Gdns EH17 ......51 B3
Greenend Gr EH17 ......51 B4
Greenhill Ct EH10 ......25 A1
Greenhill Gdns EH10 ......25 A1
Greenhill Pk EH10 ......37 A4
Greenhill Pl EH10 ......37 A4
Greenhill Terr EH10 ......25 A1
Greenlaw Hedge
EH13 ......48 A4
Greenlaw Rig EH13 ......48 A4
Greenmantle Loan 9
EH16 ......39 A1
Greenpark EH17 ......51 B4
Greenside La EH1 ......64 B4
Greenside Pl EH1 ......64 B4
Greenside Row
Edinburgh EH1 ......64 B4
Green St EH7 ......15 C2
Green, The EH4 ......12 B4
Greyfriars EH1 ......64 A2
Greyfriars Kirk★
EH1 ......65 A2
Grierson Ave EH5 ......06 C2
Grierson Cres EH5 ......06 C2
Grierson Gdns EH5 ......06 C2
Grierson Rd EH5 ......06 B2
Grierson Sq EH5 ......06 C1
Grierson Villas EH5 ......06 C1
Grigor Ave EH4 ......13 C3
Grigor Dr EH4 ......13 C3
Grigor Gdns EH4 ......14 A3
Grigor Terr EH4 ......13 C3
Grindlay St EH3 ......63 B2
Grindlay St Ct EH3 ......63 B2
Groathill Ave EH4 ......13 B2
Groathill Gdns E 2
EH4 ......13 B2

Groathill Gdns W 1
EH4 ......13 B2
Groathill Rd N EH4 ......13 B3
Groathill Rd S EH4 ......13 B2
Grosvenor Cres 24 B3
63 A2
Grosvenor Gdns
EH12 ......24 B3
Grosvenor St EH12 ......63 A2
Grove St
Edinburgh EH3 ......63 A2
Musselburgh EH21 ......31 C1
Grundie's Well Rd
EH17 ......52 A2
Guardians Wood
EH12 ......23 B3
Guardwell Cres EH17 ......51 B3
Gullan's Cl EH1 ......64 B3
Guthrie St EH1 ......65 A2
Gyle Ave EH12 ......20 B1
Gylemuir Prim Sch
EH12 ......21 B2
Gyle Par K Gdns
EH12 ......20 C2
Gyle Rdbt EH12 ......20 B1
Gyle Sh Ctr EH12 ......20 C1

H

Haddington Pl EH7 ......16 A2
Haddon's Ct EH8 ......65 B2
Hailes App EH13 ......46 C3
Hailes Bank EH13 ......46 C3
Hailes Cres EH13 ......46 C3
Hailes Gdns EH13 ......46 C3
Hailes Gr EH13 ......46 C3
Hailesland Gdns
EH14 ......34 A1
Hailesland Gr EH14 ......34 A1
Hailesland Pk EH14 ......34 A1
Hailesland Pl EH14 ......34 A1
Hailesland Prim Sch
EH14 ......46 A4
Hailesland Rd EH14 ......34 A1
Hailes Pk EH13 ......46 C3
Hailes St EH3 ......63 B1
Hailes Terr EH13 ......46 C3
Hainburn Pk EH10 ......48 B1
Hallhead Rd EH16 ......38 B2
Halmyre St EH6 ......16 B4
Hamburgh Pl EH6 ......08 A2
Hamilton Dr EH15 ......28 B3
Hamilton Dr W EH15 ......28 B3
Hamilton Gdns EH15 ......28 B3
Hamilton Pk EH15 ......28 B3
Hamilton Pl EH3 ......15 A2
Hamiltons Folly Mews
EH8 ......65 B1
Hamilton Terr EH15 ......28 C3
Hamilton Wynd EH6 ......08 A2
Hammermen's Entry
EH8 ......64 A3
Hampton Terr EH12 ......24 A3
Hanover St EH2 ......63 C4
Harbour Pl EH15 ......18 C1
Harbour Rd
Edinburgh EH15 ......18 C1
Musselburgh EH21 ......30 C2
Harden Pl EH11 ......24 B1
Hardwell Cl EH8 ......65 B2
Harelaw Rd EH13 ......47 A3
Harewood Cres EH16 ......40 A4
Harewood Dr EH16 ......40 A4
Harewood Rd EH16 ......40 A4
Harrismith Pl EH7 ......16 C2
Harrison Gdns EH11 ......36 A4
Harrison La EH11 ......24 A1
Harrison Pl EH11 ......36 A4
Harrison Rd EH11 ......24 A1
Hartington Gdns
EH10 ......24 C1
Hartington Pl EH10 ......24 C1
Hart St EH1 ......15 C2
Hart St La EH1 ......15 C2
Harvesters Way EH14 ......45 C4
Hatton Pl EH9 ......25 C1
Haugh Pk EH14 ......34 C2
Haugh St EH4 ......15 A2
Hawkhead Cres
EH16 ......50 C4
Hawkhead Gr 3
EH16 ......50 C4
Hawkhill EH7 ......17 A3
Hawkhill Ave EH7 ......16 C3
Hawthornbank La
EH4 ......62 A3
Hawthornbank Pl
EH6 ......07 C2
Hawthornbank Terr
EH6 ......08 A2
Hawthornden Pl EH6 ......16 A3
Hawthorn Gdns EH20 ......59 A1
Hawthorn Pl EH17 ......52 A2
Hawthornvale EH6 ......07 C2
Hay Ave EH16 ......40 B4

Hay Dr EH1 ......28 C1
Hayfield EH12 ......20 C4
Hay Gdns 40 B4
Edinburgh EH16 ......28 B1
Haymarket EH12 ......63 A2
Haymarket Sta EH12 ......63 A2
Haymarket Terr
Edinburgh EH12 ......24 B3
Edinburgh EH12 ......63 A2
Haymarket Yds EH12 ......63 A2
Hay Pl EH16 ......40 B4
Hay Rd EH16 ......40 B4
Hays Com Bsns Ctr
EH16 ......40 B4
Hay Terr EH16 ......40 B4
Hazelbank Terr EH11 ......36 A3
Hazeldean Terr EH16 ......39 A1
Hazelwood Gr EH16 ......40 B4
Headrigg Row EH16 ......39 A1
Henderland Rd EH12 ......23 C3
Henderson Gdns EH6 ......08 B1
Henderson Pl EH3 ......15 B2
Henderson Pl La EH3 ......15 A2
Henderson Row EH3 ......15 A2
Henderson Terr
EH11 ......24 B1
Hercus Loan EH21 ......31 A2
Heriot Bridge EH1 ......63 C2
Heriot Hill Terr EH7 ......15 B3
Heriot Pl EH3 ......63 C2
Heriot Row EH3 ......62 B4
Heriot-Watt Univ
EH14 ......44 A4
Hermand Cres EH11 ......36 A4
Hermand St EH11 ......35 C4
Hermand Terr EH11 ......35 C4
Hermiston Gait Ret Pk
EH11 ......32 C3
Hermiston Ho Rd
EH12,EH14 ......32 A2
Hermiston Junc
EH11 ......32 C2
Hermitage Dr EH10 ......37 A2
Hermitage Gdns
EH10 ......37 A2
Hermitage of Braid
Visitor Ctr★ EH10 ......37 B1
Hermitage Pk EH6 ......17 A3
Hermitage Pk Gr
EH6 ......17 A3
Hermitage Pk Lea
EH6 ......17 A3
Hermitage Pk Prim Sch
EH6 ......17 A3
Hermitage Pk S EH6 ......17 A3
Hermitage Pl EH6 ......16 C4
Hermitage Terr EH10 ......37 A2
Hermits Croft EH8 ......65 C1
High Buckstone
EH10 ......49 B2
High Kirk of St Giles★
EH1 ......64 A3
High Riggs EH3 ......63 B2
High School Wynd 64 B3
High School Yds 64 B2
High St
Bonnyrigg and Lasswade
EH18 ......60 C1
Edinburgh EH15 ......18 C1
Musselburgh EH21 ......31 C2
Hillcoat Loan EH15 ......18 C1
Hillcoat Pl EH15 ......18 C1
Hillhouse Rd
Edinburgh EH4 ......13 A2
Edinburgh EH4 ......13 C2
Hillpark Ave EH4 ......12 B1
Hillpark Brae EH4 ......12 B1
Hillpark Cres EH4 ......12 B1
Hillpark Ct EH4 ......12 B3
Hillpark Dr EH4 ......12 B3
Hillpark Gdns EH4 ......12 B2
Hillpark Gn EH4 ......12 B2
Hillpark Gr EH4 ......12 B2
Hillpark Loan EH4 ......12 C2
Hillpark Rd EH4 ......12 B2
Hillpark Terr EH4 ......12 B2
Hillpark Way EH4 ......12 C2
Hillpark Wood EH4 ......12 C2
Hill Pl EH8 ......65 B2
Hillside Cres EH7 ......16 A2
Hillside St EH7 ......16 A2
Hill Sq EH8 ......65 B2
Hill St EH2 ......63 B4
Hill St La N EH2 ......63 B3
Hill St La S EH2 ......63 B3
Hillview EH4 ......13 A2
Hillview Cres EH12 ......21 C3
Hillview Dr EH12 ......21 B3
Hillview Rd EH12 ......21 C3
Hillview Terr EH12 ......21 C3
Hollybank Terr EH11 ......36 A4
Holy Cross RC Prim Sch
EH6 ......7 B1
Holyrood Bsns Pk
EH16 ......39 C4
Holyrood Pk Rd
Edinburgh EH16 ......26 B1

Holyrood Pk Rd continued
Edinburgh EH16 ......65 C1
Holy Rood RC High Sch
EH15 ......27 C1
Holyrood Rd EH8 ......64 C3
Home St EH3 ......63 B1
Hopefield Terr EH6 ......08 A2
Hope La EH15 ......29 A3
Hope La N EH15 ......29 A4
Hope Pk Cres EH8 ......65 B1
Hope Pk Sq EH8 ......65 B1
Hope Pk Terr EH8 ......65 B1
Hope St EH2 ......62 B3
Hope St La EH2 ......62 B3
Hope Terr EH9 ......37 B4
Hopetoun Cres EH7 ......16 A2
Hopetoun St EH7 ......16 A2
Horne Terr EH11 ......63 A1
Horse Wynd EH8 ......64 C3
Hoseason Gdns EH4 ......11 C1
Hosie Rigg EH15 ......29 A1
House O'hill Ave EH4 ......12 C3
House O'hill Brae
EH4 ......12 C3
House O'hill Cres
EH4 ......12 C3
House O'hill Gdns
EH4 ......13 A3
House O'hill Gn EH4 ......12 C3
House O'hill Gr EH4 ......12 C3
House O'hill Rd EH4 ......13 A3
House O'hill Row
EH4 ......13 A3
House O'hill Terr
EH4 ......13 A2
Howard Pl EH3 ......15 B3
Howard St EH3 ......15 B3
Howden H Cres EH16 ......50 B2
Howden H Ct EH16 ......50 B2
Howden H Dr
EH16 ......50 B2
Howden H Gdns
EH16 ......50 C2
Howden H Loan
EH16 ......50 C2
Howden H Pk EH16 ......50 B2
Howden H Rd EH16 ......50 C1
Howden H Way EH16 ......50 C1
Howden St EH8 ......65 B2
Howe St EH3 ......15 B2
Hugh Miller Pl EH3 ......14 C2
Hunter's Cl EH1 ......63 C2
Hunter Sq EH1 ......64 A3
Hunter's Tryst Prim Sch
EH13 ......48 B3
Huntingdon Pl EH7 ......16 A2
Huntly St EH3 ......15 B3
Hutchison Ave EH14 ......35 B3
Hutchison Cotts
EH14 ......35 B3
Hutchison Crossway
EH14 ......35 B4
Hutchison Gdns
EH14 ......35 B3
Hutchison Loan EH14 ......35 B3
Hutchison Medway
EH14 ......35 B3
Hutchison Pk EH14 ......35 B4
Hutchison Pl EH14 ......35 B3
Hutchison Terr EH14 ......35 B3
Hutchison View EH14 ......35 B4
Hyot Ave EH17 ......51 C2
Hyot Bank Ave EH17 ......52 A2
Hyot Ct EH17 ......51 C1
Hyot Gdns EH17 ......51 C2
Hyot Gn EH17 ......51 C1
Hyot Gr EH17 ......51 C2
Hyot Loan EH17 ......51 C2
Hyot Pk EH17 ......51 C2
Hyot Terr EH17 ......51 C1
Hyot View EH17 ......51 C1

I

Inchview Prim Sch
EH4 ......13 B4
Inchview Terr EH7 ......18 B1
India Pl EH3 ......62 B4
India St EH3 ......62 B4
Industrial Rd EH6 ......16 C4
Industry La EH6 ......08 A1
Infirmary St EH1 ......65 B2
Inglewood Pl 7
EH16 ......51 A4
Inglis Ct EH1 ......63 C2
Inglis Gn Rd EH14 ......35 A2
Inglis Gn Rigg EH14 ......35 A2
Inveralmond Dr EH4 ......02 C1
Inveralmond Gdns
EH4 ......02 C1
Inveralmond Gr EH4 ......02 C1
Inveravon Rd EH20 ......59 A1
Inveravon Terr EH21 ......31 B1
Inveresk Brae EH21 ......31 C1

Inveresk Est, The
EH21 ......43 C4
Inveresk Gate EH21 ......31 C1
Inveresk Ind Est
EH21 ......31 B1
Inveresk Lodge Gdn★
EH21 ......43 C4
Inveresk Mills Ind Pk
EH21 ......31 A1
Inveresk Rd EH21 ......31 B1
Inveresk Village Rd 43
......43 C1
Inverleith Ave S EH3 ......14 C4
Inverleith Gdns EH3 ......14 C4
Inverleith Gr EH3 ......14 B3
Inverleith Pl EH3 ......14 B3
Inverleith Pl La EH3 ......14 C4
Inverleith Row EH3 ......15 A4
Inverleith Terr EH3 ......14 C3
Inverleith Terr La
EH3 ......15 A3
Iona St EH6 ......16 B3
Ivanhoe Cres EH16 ......39 A1
Ivy Terr EH11 ......24 A1

J

Jamaica Mews EH3 ......62 B4
Jamaica St EH3 ......62 B4
Jamaica St N La 62 B4
Jamaica St S La 62 B4
Jamaica St W EH3 ......62 B4
James Gillespie's High
Sch EH9 ......25 B1
James Gillespie's Prim
Sch EH9 ......25 B1
Jameson Pl EH6 ......16 B3
James St
Edinburgh EH15 ......29 B4
Musselburgh EH21 ......31 C2
James St La EH15 ......29 B4
Janefield EH17 ......58 C4
Jane St EH6 ......16 B4
Jean Armour Ave 6
EH16 ......38 C1
Jeffrey Ave EH4 ......13 A1
Jeffrey St EH1 ......64 B3
Jessfield Terr EH6 ......07 C2
Jewel & Esk Valley Coll
EH15 ......29 B2
Jewel, The EH15 ......29 A1
John Cotton Bsns Ctr
EH7 ......16 C2
Johnston Terr EH1 ......63 C2
Joppa Gdns EH15 ......29 B3
Joppa Gr EH15 ......29 B3
Joppa Pk EH15 ......29 B3
Joppa Rd EH15 ......29 B3
Joppa Terr EH15 ......29 B3
Jordan La EH10 ......37 A3
Junction Pl
Edinburgh EH6 ......08 B1
Edinburgh EH6 ......16 B4

Juniper Ave EH14 ......45 B2
Juniper Gdns EH14 ......45 B2
Juniper Gn Prim Sch
EH14 ......45 C2
Juniper La EH14 ......45 B2
Juniperlee EH14 ......45 C1
Juniper Pk Rd EH14 ......45 B2
Juniper Terr EH14 ......45 C2

K

Kaimes Rd EH12 ......22 B3
Kaimes Specl Sch
EH16 ......51 B2
Kaimes View EH22 ......53 A3
Katesmill Rd EH14 ......47 A4
Kedslie Pl EH16 ......50 B3
Kedslie Rd EH16 ......50 B3
Keir St EH3 ......63 C2
Keith Cres EH4 ......13 A1
Keith Row EH4 ......13 B1
Keith Terr EH4 ......13 A1
Kekewich Ave EH7 ......18 B2
Kemp Pl EH3 ......15 A2
Kemp's Cnr EH7 ......17 C2
Kenilworth Dr EH16 ......51 A4
Kenmure Ave EH8 ......27 B4
Kerr St EH3 ......15 A2
Kerr's Wynd EH21 ......31 C2
Kew Terr EH12 ......23 C3
Kilchurn Ct EH12 ......20 C3
Kilgraston Rd EH9 ......25 B1
Killwinning St EH21 ......31 C2
Killwinning Terr
EH21 ......31 C2

Kilmaurs Rd EH16 ......38 C4
Kilmaurs Terr EH16 ......38 C4
Kilncroftside EH14 ......35 A2
Kingate Brae EH17 ......51 C1
Kilwinning Pl EH21 ......31 B2
Kinellan Gdns EH12 ......23 B4
Kinellan Rd EH12 ......23 B4
Kinghorn Pl EH6 ......07 C1
King Malcolm Cl
EH10 ......49 C1
Kingsburgh Rd EH12 ......23 B3
Kings Cramond EH4 ......03 A1
Kings Haugh EH16 ......39 B4
Kingsinch Specl Sch
EH16 ......38 C2
Kingsknowe Ave
EH14 ......34 C1
Kingsknowe Cres
EH14 ......34 C1
Kingsknowe Ct EH14 ......34 B1
Kingsknowe Dr EH14 ......34 C1
Kingsknowe Gdns
EH14 ......46 C4
Kingsknowe Pk EH14 ......46 C4
Kingsknowe Pl EH14 ......34 C1
Kingsknowe Rd N
EH14 ......34 C2
Kingsknowe Rd S
EH14 ......34 C1
Kingsknowe Sta
EH14 ......34 C1
Kingsknowe Terr
EH14 ......34 C1
King's Mdw EH16 ......39 A4
King's Rd EH15 ......18 C1
King's Stables La EH1 ......63 C2
King's Stables Rd
Edinburgh EH1 ......62 B2
King St Edinburgh EH6 ......08 B1
Musselburgh EH21 ......31 C1
King's Terr EH15 ......18 C1
Kingston Ave EH16 ......39 B1
Kinnaird Pk EH15 ......41 B4
Kinnear Rd EH3 ......14 C4
Kirk Brae
Edinburgh EH16 ......38 C2
Edinburgh EH16 ......50 C4
Kirk Cramond EH4 ......03 B2
Kirkgate
Edinburgh EH16 ......50 C3
Edinburgh EH6 ......08 C1
Kirkhill Dr EH16 ......26 C1
Kirkhill Gdns EH16 ......26 C1
Kirkhill Rd EH16 ......26 C1
Kirkhill Terr EH16 ......26 C1
Kirklands EH12 ......33 C4
Kirk Loan EH12 ......22 A2
Kirk Pk EH16 ......50 C4
Kirk St EH6 ......16 B4
Kisimul Ct EH12 ......21 A3
Kittle Yds 26 A1
Klondyke St EH15 ......42 A4
Kyle Pl EH7 ......64 C4

L

Ladehead EH6 ......15 C4
Ladiemeadow EH12 ......22 A1
Lady Lawson St EH3 ......63 C2
Lady Menzies Pl 3
EH7 ......16 C2
Lady Nairne Cres
EH8 ......27 C3
Lady Nairne Gr EH8 ......27 C3
Lady Nairne Loan
EH8 ......27 C3
Lady Nairne Pl EH8 ......27 C3
Lady Rd EH16 ......38 C2
Ladysmith Rd EH9 ......38 A2
Ladywell EH21 ......31 B2
Ladywell Ave EH12 ......21 C1
Ladywell Ct EH12 ......21 C1
Ladywell Gdns EH12 ......21 C1
Ladywell Rd EH12 ......21 B2
Ladywell Way EH21 ......31 B2
Lady Wynd EH1 ......63 C2
Laichfield EH14 ......35 A3
Laichpark Pl EH14 ......35 A3
Laichpark Rd EH14 ......35 A3
Laing Terr EH15 ......29 B4
Lamb's Cl EH8 ......65 B1
Lambs Ct EH6 ......07 B3
Lammermoor Terr
EH16 ......51 C4
Lampacre Rd EH12 ......22 A1
Lanark Rd
Edinburgh, Kingsknowe
EH14 ......35 A1
Edinburgh, Westerhailes
EH13, EH14 ......46 A2
Lang Loan 59 A2
Loanhead EH17,EH20 ......59 B3
Langton Rd EH9 ......38 A3

Lansdowne Cres
Edinburgh EH12 ....24 B3
Edinburgh EH12 ....63 A2
Lapicide Pl EH6 ....08 A1
Larbourfield EH11 ....33 C1
Largo Pl EH6 ....08 A1
Larkfield Dr EH22 .....61 C1
Lasswade Bank EH17 ..51 B1
Lasswade Gr EH17 ....51 B1
Lasswade Rd
Bonnyrigg and Lasswade
EH18 ....60 C1
Dalkeith EH22 ....61 C2
Edinburgh EH16, EH17,
EH18 ....51 B2
Latch Pk EH13 ....47 B3
Lauderdale St EH9 ....25 B1
Lauder Loan EH9 .....37 C4
Lauder Rd EH9 ....37 C4
Laura Fergusson Ct
EH12 ....11 A1
Laurel Terr EH11 ......24 A1
Laurie St
Edinburgh EH6 ....08 C1
Edinburgh EH6 ....16 C4
Lauriston Castle★
EH4 ....4 A1
Lauriston Farm Rd
EH4 ....12 A4
Lauriston Gdns EH3 ...63 C1
Lauriston Pk EH3 .....63 C1
Lauriston Pl
Edinburgh EH3 ....63 C2
Edinburgh EH3 ....65 A2
Lauriston St EH3 ......63 C2
Lauriston Terr EH3 ....63 C2
Laverockbank Ave
EH5 ....07 B2
Laverockbank Cres
EH5 ....07 B2
Laverock Bank Gdns ..07 B2
Laverockbank Gr
EH5 ....07 B2
Laverockbank Rd
EH5 ....07 B2
Laverockbank Terr
EH5 ....07 B2
Laverockdale Cres
EH13 ....47 A1
Laverockdale Loan
EH13 ....47 A1
Laverockdale Pk
EH13 ....47 A1
Lawhouse Toll EH15 ...41 A4
Lawnmarket EH1 ......64 A3
Law Pl EH15 ....18 C1
Leadervale Rd EH16 ...50 B4
Leadervale Terr
EH16 ....50 B4
Leamington Pl EH10 ...63 B1
Leamington Rd EH3 ...63 A1
Leamington Terr
Edinburgh EH10 ....25 A1
Edinburgh EH10 ....63 B1
Learmonth Ave EH4 ...14 B2
Learmonth Cres EH4 ..14 B2
Learmonth Ct EH4 ....14 B1
Learmonth Gd EH4 ....62 A4
Learmonth Gdns EH4 ..14 B1
Learmonth Gdns Mews
[11] Edinburgh EH4 ......14 C2
Edinburgh EH4 ....62 A4
Learmonth Gr EH4 ....14 B2
Learmonth Pl EH4 ....62 A4
Learmonth Terr
Edinburgh EH4 ....14 B1
Edinburgh EH4 ....62 A4
Learmonth Terr La
EH4 ....62 A4
Leith Acad EH6 ....16 C3
Leith Prim Sch EH6 ...16 C4
Leith St EH1 ....64 A4
Leith Waterworld★
EH6 ....16 C4
Leith Wlk EH6,EH7 .....16 B3
Leith Wlk Prim Sch
EH7 ....16 A2
Lennel Ave EH12 ......23 B4
Lennox Row EH5 ......07 A2
Lennox St EH4 ....62 A4
Lennox St La EH4 .....62 A4
Leopold Pl [6] EH7 ....16 A2
Leslie Pl EH4 ....14 C2
Leven Cl EH3 ....63 B1
Leven St EH3 ....63 B1
Leven Terr EH3 ....63 C1
Lewis Terr EH11 ......63 A2
Liberton Brae
Edinburgh EH16 ....38 C1
Edinburgh EH16 ....50 C4
Liberton Dr
Edinburgh EH16 ....50 B4
Edinburgh EH16 ....50 C3
Liberton Gdns EH16 ...50 C2
Liberton High Sch
EH17 ....51 B4
Liberton Hospl EH16 ..50 C3
Liberton Pl EH16 ......50 C3
Liberton Prim Sch
EH16 ....38 C2
Liberton Rd EH16 .....38 C1
Liddesdale Pl EH3 ....15 A2
Lilyhill Terr
Edinburgh EH8 ....17 B1
Edinburgh EH8 ....27 B4
Lily Terr EH11 ....36 A4
Limefield EH17 ....52 A1
Limes, The EH10 ......36 C4
Lindean Pl EH6 ....17 A4
Lindsay Pl EH6 ....08 A2
Lindsay Rd
Edinburgh EH6 ....07 C2
Edinburgh EH6 ....08 A2
Lindsay St EH6 ....08 A2
Linkfield Rd EH21 .....31 C2
Links Ave EH21 ....31 A3
Links Gdns EH6 ....09 A1
Links Gdns La EH6 ....09 A1
Links Pl EH6 ....08 C1
Links St EH21 ....31 B2
Links View EH21 ......31 A3
Lismore Ave [4] EH8 ...17 B1
Lismore Cres
Edinburgh EH8 ....17 B1
Edinburgh EH8 ....27 B4
Lismore Prim Sch
EH15 ....28 B1
Little France Mills
EH16 ....39 C1
Littlejohn Rd EH10 ....48 A4
Little King St EH1 ....64 A4
Little Rd EH16 ....51 A3
Livingstone Pl EH9 ....25 C1
Lixmount Ave EH5 .....07 B2
Lixmount Gdns EH5 ...07 B2
Loanhead Rd EH20 ....58 C2
Loaning Cres EH7 .....17 C2
Loaning Rd EH7 ....17 C2
Lochend Ave EH7 .....17 A3
Lochend Castle Barns
EH7 ....17 A2
Lochend Cl EH8 ....64 C3
Lochend Cres EH7 ....17 B2
Lochend Dr EH7 ....17 A2
Lochend Gdns EH7 ....17 A2
Lochend Gr EH7 ....17 B2
Lochend Pk EH7 ....17 A2
Lochend Quadrant
EH7 ....17 B2
Lochend Rd EH6, EH7 ..16 C3
Lochend Rd N EH21 ...31 A2
Lochend Rd S
Edinburgh EH7 ....17 A2
Musselburgh EH21 .....31 A2
Lochend Sq EH7 ......17 A2
Loch Rd EH4 ....12 C2
Lochrin Bldgs EH3 ....63 B1
Lochrin Pl EH3 ....63 B1
Lochrin Terr EH3 ......63 B1
Lochside Ave EH12 ....32 B4
Lochside Cres EH12 ...32 B4
Lochside Ct EH12 .....32 C4
Lochside Pl EH12 ......32 C4
Lochside View EH12 ...20 B1
Lochside Way EH12 ...32 C4
Lockerby Cotts EH16 ..51 B2
Lockerby Cres EH16 ...51 B2
Lockerby Gr EH16 .....51 B2
Lockharton Ave
EH14 ....35 C2
Lockharton Cres
EH14 ....36 A2
Lockharton Gdns
EH14 ....36 A3
Loganlea Ave EH7 .....17 C2
Loganlea Dr EH7 ......17 C2
Loganlea Gdns EH7 ...17 B2
Loganlea Loan EH7 ...17 C1
Loganlea Pl EH7 ....17 C1
Loganlea Rd EH7 ......17 C2
Loganlea Terr EH7 ....17 C2
Logan St EH3 ....15 B2
Logie Gn Gdns EH7 ...15 B3
Logie Gn Rd EH7 ......15 B3
Logie Mill EH7 ....15 B3
Lomond Rd EH5 ....07 A2
Lomond Wlk EH20 .....58 C1
London Rd
Edinburgh EH7 ....16 B1
Edinburgh EH7, EH8 ....17 A1
London St EH3 ....15 C2
Long Craig Rigg EH5 ..05 B3
Longformacus Rd
EH16 ....50 C3
Longstone Ave EH14 ..34 C2
Longstone Cres
EH14 ....34 C2
Longstone Gdns
EH14 ....34 B3
Longstone Gr EH14 ...34 C2
Longstone Pk EH14 ...34 C2
Longstone Pl EH14 ....34 C2
Longstone Prim Sch
EH14 ....34 C1
Longstone Rd
Edinburgh EH14 ....34 B3
Edinburgh EH14 ....34 C2
Longstone St EH14 ...34 C2
Longstone Terr EH14 ..34 B3
Longstone View
EH14 ....34 B3
Lonsdale Terr EH3 .....63 C1
Loretto Ct EH21 ....43 A4
Loretto Jun Sch
EH21 ....31 B2
Loretto RC Prim Sch
EH21 ....31 C2
Loretto Schs EH21 ....31 C2
Lorimer View EH14 ....46 A2
Lorne Gr EH20 ....58 C1
Lorne Pl EH6 ....16 B3
Lorne Prim Sch EH6 ..16 B3
Lorne Sq EH6 ....16 B3
Lorne St EH6 ....16 B3
Lothian Rd EH1 ....63 B2
Lothian St EH1 ....65 A2
Lower Gilmore Pl
EH3 ....63 A1
Lower Granton Rd 06 C3
Edinburgh EH5 ....06 B3
Lower Joppa EH15 ....29 B4
Lower London Rd
EH7 ....16 C1
Lussielaw Rd EH9 .....38 B2
Lutton Ct Bsns Ctr
EH8 ....65 B1
Lutton Pl EH8 ....65 B1
Lygon Rd
Edinburgh EH16 ....38 B2
Edinburgh EH16 ....38 C2
Lynedoch Pl EH3 ......62 A3
Lynedoch Pl La EH3 ...62 A3
Lyne St EH7 ....16 C1

M

Macdowall Rd EH9 ....38 A3
Mackenzie Pl EH3 .....62 B4
Madeira Pl EH6 ....08 A1
Madeira St EH6 ....08 A2
Magdala Cres EH12 ....24 B3
Magdala Mews EH12 ..24 B3
Magdalene Ave EH15 ..29 A2
Magdalene Ct EH15 ...29 A2
Magdalene Dr EH15 ...29 A2
Magdalene Gdns
EH15 ....29 A2
Magdalene Loan
EH15 ....29 A2
Magdalene Medway
EH15 ....29 A2
Magdalene Pl EH15 ...29 A2
Maidencraig Cres
EH4 ....13 B2
Maidencraig Gr EH4 ...13 B2
Main Point EH3 ....63 C2
Mains Of Craigmillar
EH16 ....39 C2
Main St EH4 ....12 B3
Maitland Ave EH21 ....30 C2
Maitland Pk Rd EH21 ..30 C2
Maitland St EH21 ......30 C2
Malbet Pk EH16 ....51 A3
Malbet Wynd EH16 ....51 A3
Mall Ave EH21 ....31 B1
Malta Gn EH4 ....15 A2
Malta Terr EH4 ....15 A2
Manderston St EH6 ....16 B4
Mannering Pl [9]
EH16 ....51 A4
Manor Pl EH3 ....62 A3
Manse La EH21 ....31 C2
Manse Rd EH12 ....21 C2
Manse St EH12 ....21 C2
Mansfield Ave EH21 ...31 B2
Mansfield Ct EH21 ....31 C1
Mansfield Pl
Edinburgh EH3 ....15 C2
Musselburgh EH21 .....31 B1
Mansfield Rd EH21 ....31 B2
Mansionhouse Rd
EH9 ....25 C1
Marchfield Gr EH4 ....12 C3
Marchfield Pk EH4 ....12 B3
Marchfield Pk La
EH4 ....12 B3
Marchfield Terr EH4 ...12 C3
March Gait EH4 ....12 B2
March Gr EH4 ....12 C2
Marchhall Cres EH16 ..26 C1
Marchhall Pl EH16 ....26 C1
Marchhall Rd EH16 ....26 C1
Marchmont Cres
EH9 ....25 C1
Marchmont Rd EH9 ....25 B1
Marchmont St EH9 ....25 B1
Marchmount Cres 63 C1
Marchmount Rd 63 C1
March Pines EH4 ......12 B2
March Rd EH4 ....12 C2
Mardale Cres EH10 ....36 C4
Marine Dr 04 B2
Marine Espl EH6 ....09 B1
Marionville Ave EH7 ...17 A2
Marionville Cres EH7 ..17 B2
Marionville Dr EH7 ....17 B2
Marionville Gr EH7 ....17 B2
Marionville Pk EH7 ....17 A2
Marionville Rd EH7 ....17 A1
Marischal Pl [7] EH4 ...13 B2
Maritime La EH6 ....08 C1
Maritime St EH6 ....08 C1
Market St
Edinburgh EH1 ....64 A3
Musselburgh EH21 .....31 A2
Marlborough St
EH15 ....29 A4
Marmion Cres EH16 ...39 A1
Marshall's Ct EH1 .....64 B4
Marshall St EH8 ....65 A2
Mary Erskine Sch The
EH4 ....13 A1
Mary Erskine & Stewart's
Melville Jun Sch The
EH4 ....14 B1
Maryfield [2] EH7 ......16 B2
Mary Field EH15 ....19 A1
Maryfield Pl [2] EH7 ...16 C2
Mary's Pl EH4 ....14 C2
Maulsford Ave EH22 ...53 A3
Maurice Pl EH9 ....37 C2
Maxwell St EH10 ....36 C3
Maybank Villas EH12 ..21 C3
Mayburn Ave EH20 ....59 A1
Mayburn Cres EH20 ...59 A1
Mayburn Dr EH20 .....59 A1
Mayburn Loan EH20 ...59 A1
Mayburn Terr EH20 ...59 A1
Maybury Dr 11 A1
Edinburgh EH12 ....20 C4
Maybury Rd
Edinburgh EH12 ....10 C1
Edinburgh EH12 ....20 C4
Mayfield Ave EH21 ....43 A3
Mayfield Cres EH21 ...43 A4
Mayfield Gdns EH9 ....38 B4
Mayfield Gdns La
EH9 ....38 B4
Mayfield Pk EH21 .....43 A3
Mayfield Pl
Edinburgh EH12 ....21 C2
Musselburgh EH21 .....43 A3
Mayfield Rd
Edinburgh EH1 ....38 C1
Edinburgh EH9 ....38 B3
Mayfield Terr EH9 .....38 B4
Mayshade Rd EH20 ....59 A1
Mayville Gdns EH5 ....07 B2
Mayville Gdns E EH5 ..07 B2
Mcdonald Pl EH7 ......15 C3
Mcdonald Rd EH7 .....16 A3
Mcdonald St EH7 ......16 A3
Mclaren Rd EH9 ....38 C4
Mclaren Terr EH11 ....63 A2
Mcleod St EH11 ....24 A2
Mcneill St EH11 ....63 A1
Meadowbank EH8 .....17 A1
Meadowbank Ave [13]
EH8 ....17 A1
Meadowbank Cr 17 A1
Meadowbank Pl [15]
EH8 ....17 A1
Meadow Bank Sh Pk
EH8 ....16 C2
Meadowbank Sports Ctr
EH7 ....17 A1
Meadowfield Ave
EH8 ....27 C3
Meadow Field Ct
EH8 ....27 C3
Meadowfield Dr EH8 ..27 C3
Meadowfield Gdns
EH8 ....27 C2
Meadowfield Rd
EH12 ....20 A3
Meadowfield Terr
EH8 ....27 C2
Meadowhouse Rd
EH12 ....22 A2
Meadow La EH8 ....65 A1
Meadow Pl EH9 ....63 C1
Meadow Pl Rd EH12 ...21 B1
Meadow Rd EH14 ......44 B3
Meadowspot EH10 ....36 A2
Meadows, The★
EH8 ....65 A1
Mearenside EH12 ......20 C4
Meggetland Terr
EH14 ....36 A3
Melgund Terr EH7 .....15 C2
Melville Cotts EH18 ...61 B4
Melville Cres EH3 .....62 A3
Melville Dr
Edinburgh EH9 ....63 C1
Edinburgh EH9 ....65 A1
Melville Dykes Rd
EH18 ....61 A1
Melville Dykes Rd Rdbt
EH22 ....61 C2
Melville Gate EH22 ....61 C3
Melville Gate Rd
EH22 ....61 C3
Melville St EH3 ....62 A3
Melville St La EH3 .....62 A3
Melville Terr EH9 ......65 B1
Melville View EH18 ....60 C1
Mentone Ave EH15 ....19 A1
Mentone Gdns EH9 ....38 B4
Mentone Terr EH9 .....38 B3
Merchant St EH1 ......65 A2
Merchiston Ave
EH10 ....24 C1
Merchiston Bk Av
EH10 ....36 C4
Merchiston Castle Sch
EH14 ....47 A3
Merchiston Cres
EH10 ....36 C4
Merchiston Gdns
EH10 ....36 B3
Merchiston Gr EH11 ...24 A1
Merchiston Mews
EH10 ....24 C1
Merchiston Pk EH10 ...24 C1
Merchiston Pl
Edinburgh EH10 ....24 C1
Edinburgh EH10 ....36 C4
Mertoun Pl EH11 ......24 B1
Meuse La EH2 ....64 A3
Middleby Ct EH9 ......38 B4
Middleby St EH9 ......38 B4
Middlefield EH7 ....16 A3
Middleknowe EH14 ....45 B4
Middle Mdw Wlk
EH8 ....65 A1
Middlepark EH14 ......45 B4
Middleshot EH14 ......45 B4
Mid Gogarloch Syke
EH12 ....20 C1
Mid Liberton EH16 ....38 C2
Midmar Ave EH10 .....37 B2
Midmar Dr EH10 ......37 B2
Midmar Gdns EH10 ...37 A2
Mid New Cultins
EH11 ....32 C2
Mid Steil EH10 ....36 A1
Millar Cres EH10 ......36 C3
Millar Pl EH10 ....36 C3
Millar Pl La EH10 .....36 C3
Millbrae Wynd EH14 ...35 A2
Millerfield Pl EH9 .....25 C1
Millerhill Rd
Dalkeith EH22 ....41 A2
Dalkeith EH22 ....53 C1
Miller Row EH4 ....62 A3
Millhill EH21 ....31 C2
Millhill La EH21 ....31 C2
Millhill Wynd EH21 ....31 C2
Mill La EH6 ....08 B1
Miln-acre EH6 ....15 C4
Milton Cres EH15 ......28 C2
Milton Dr EH15 ....29 C3
Milton Gdns N EH15 ...28 C2
Milton Gdns S EH15 ...28 C2
Milton Glen EH15 .....30 A3
Milton Gr EH15 ....30 A3
Milton Link EH15 .....29 B2
Milton Rd EH15 ....29 A2
Milton Rd E EH15 .....29 C3
Milton Rd W
Edinburgh EH15 ....28 A2
Edinburgh EH15 ....28 C2
Milton St EH8 ....16 C1
Milton Terr EH15 .....30 A3
Minto St EH9 ....26 B1
Mitchell St EH6 ....08 C1
Moat Dr EH14 ....35 C4
Moat Pl EH14 ....35 C4
Moat St EH14 ....35 C4
Moat Terr EH14 ....35 C4
Moira Pk EH7 ....18 A1
Moira Terr EH7 ....18 A1
Moira Terr La EH7 .....18 A1
Moncrieff Terr EH9 ....26 A1
Monkbarns Gdns [8]
EH16 ....51 A4
Monktonhall Pl EH21 ..43 A3
Monktonhall Terr
EH21 ....43 A4
Monkwood Ct EH9 ....37 C4
Monmouth Terr
Edinburgh EH3 ....15 A4
Edinburgh EH5 ....07 A1
Montague St EH8 ......65 B1
Montagu Terr EH3 ....15 A4
Montgomery St EH7 ...16 B2
Montgomery St La
EH7 ....16 A2
Montpelier EH10 ......24 C1
Montpelier Pk EH10 ...24 C1
Montpelier Tr 24 C1
Montrose Terr [8]
EH7 ....16 C1
Montrose Tr 64 C4
Moorfield Cotts EH22 .53 B4
Moray Ho Coll of Ed
Edinburgh, Canongate
EH8 ....64 B3
Edinburgh, Cramond EH4 ..3 B2
Moray Pk Terr EH7 ....16 C2
Moray Pl EH3 ....62 B4
Moredun EH17 ....52 A3
Moredun Dykes Rd
EH17 ....51 C2
Moredun Pk Ct EH17 ..51 C3
Moredun Pk Dr EH17 ..51 C3
Moredun Pk Gdns
EH17 ....51 C3
Moredun Pk Gn
EH17 ....52 A3
Moredun Pk Loan
EH17 ....51 C3
Moredun Pk Rd EH17 .52 A4
Moredun Pk St EH17 ..51 C3
Moredun Pk View
EH17 ....52 A3
Moredun Pk Way
EH17 ....51 C3
Moredun Pk Wlk
EH17 ....52 A3
Moredun Prim Sch
EH17 ....51 C4
Moredunvale Bank
EH17 ....51 C4
Moredunvale Gn
EH17 ....51 C4
Moredunvale Gr
EH17 ....51 C4
Moredunvale Loan
EH17 ....51 C4
Moredunvale Pk
EH17 ....51 C4
Moredunvale Pl
EH17 ....51 C4
Moredunvale Rd
Edinburgh EH17 ....39 C1
Edinburgh EH17 ....51 C4
Moredunvale View
EH17 ....51 C4
Moredunvale Way
EH17 ....51 C4
Morham Gait EH10 ....48 A4
Morham Lea EH10 ....48 A4
Morham Pk EH10 .....48 A4
Morningside Ct EH10 ..36 C2
Morningside Dr EH10 .36 B2
Morningside Gdns
EH10 ....36 B2
Morningside Gr EH10 .36 B1
Morningside Pk
EH10 ....36 C3
Morningside Pl EH10 ..36 C3
Morningside Rd
EH10 ....37 A3
Morningside Terr
EH10 ....36 C3
Morrison Cir EH3 .....63 A2
Morrison Cres EH3 ....63 A2
Morrison Link EH3 ....63 A2
Morrison St EH3 ......63 A2
Mortonhall Gate
EH16 ....50 A1
Mortonhall Pk Ave
EH17 ....50 B1
Mortonhall Pk Bank
EH17 ....50 C1
Mortonhall Pk Cres
EH17 ....50 C1
Mortonhall Pk Dr
EH17 ....50 C1
Mortonhall Pk Gdns
EH17 ....50 B1
Mortonhall Pk Gn
EH17 ....50 B1
Mortonhall Pk Gr
EH17 ....50 B1
Mortonhall Pk Loan
EH17 ....50 B1
Mortonhall Pk Pl
EH17 ....50 C1
Mortonhall Pk Terr
EH17 ....50 C1
Mortonhall Pk View
EH17 ....50 B1
Mortonhall Pk Way
EH17 ....50 B1
Mortonhall Rd EH9 ....37 C3
Morton St EH15 ....29 B3
Morvenside EH14 .....45 B4
Morvenside Cl EH14 ...45 B4
Morven St EH4 ....11 B1
Mossgiel Wlk [4]
EH16 ....38 C1
Moston Terr EH9 .....38 B4
Mound Pl EH1 ....62 C3
Mound, The 62 C3
Mount Alvernia EH16 ..51 A3
Mountcastle Bank
EH8 ....28 B4
Mountcastle Cres
EH8 ....28 A4
Mountcastle Dr N
EH15 ....28 A4

Mountcastle Dr S
EH15 ...... 28 C2
Mountcastle Gdns
EH8 ...... 28 A4
Mountcastle Gn 1
EH8 ...... 18 A1
Mount Castle Gr ...28 A4
Mountcastle Loan
EH8 ...... 18 A1
Mountcastle Pk 3
EH8 ...... 18 A1
Mountcastle Pl 2
EH8 ...... 18 A1
Mountcastle Terr
EH8 ...... 28 A4
Mount Grange EH9 ...37 B4
Mounthooly Loan
EH10 ...... 49 C1
Mount Lodge Pl
EH15 ...... 29 A4
Mount Vernon Rd
EH16 ...... 51 A4
Mucklets Ave EH21 ...42 C4
Mucklets Cres EH21 ...42 C3
Mucklets Ct EH21 ...42 C4
Mucklets Dr EH21 ...42 C4
Mucklets Pl EH21 ...42 C4
Mucklets Rd EH21 ...42 B3
Muirdale Terr EH4 ...13 A2
Muirend Ave EH14 ...46 A3
Muirhouse Ave EH4 ...13 A4
Muirhouse Ave N
EH4 ...... 13 A4
Muirhouse Bank EH4 ...13 A4
Muirhouse Cl EH4 ...12 C4
Muirhouse Cres ...05 A1
Muirhouse Dr EH4 ...04 C1
Muirhouse Gdns EH4 ...04 C1
Muirhouse Gn EH4 ...13 A4
Muirhouse Grn EH4 ...04 C1
Muirhouse Loan EH4 ...05 A1
Muirhouse Medway
Edinburgh EH4 ...... 04 C1
Edinburgh EH4 ...... 12 C4
Muirhouse Parkway
Edinburgh EH4 ...... 04 C1
Edinburgh EH4 ...... 05 A1
Muirhouse Pk EH4 ...12 C4
Muirhouse Pl E EH4 ...13 A4
Muirhouse Pl W EH4 ...13 A4
Muirhouse Prim Sch
EH4 ...... 12 C4
Muirhouse View EH4 ...04 C1
Muirhouse Way ...13 A4
Muir Wood Cres
...... 45 A1
Muir Wood Dr EH14 ...45 A1
Muir Wood Gr EH14 ...45 A1
Muir Wood Pl EH14 ...45 A1
Muir Wood Rd EH14 ...45 A1
Mulberry Pl EH6 ...07 C1
Munro Dr EH13 ...46 C1
Murano Pl EH7 ...16 B2
Murchiston Bank Gdns
EH10 ...... 36 C4
Murdoch Terr EH11 ...63 A1
Murieston Cres EH11 ...24 A2
Murieston Cres La
...... 24 B2
Murieston La EH11 ...24 A1
Murieston Pl EH11 ...24 A2
Murieston Rd EH11 ...24 A2
Murieston Terr EH11 ...24 A2
Murrayburn App
EH11 ...... 33 C1
Murrayburn Dr EH11 ...33 B1
Murrayburn Gate
EH14 ...... 45 C4
Murrayburn Gdns
...... 34 A1
Murrayburn Gn EH14 ...34 A1
Murrayburn Gr EH14 ...34 A1
Murrayburn Junc
...... 46 A3
Murrayburn Pl
Edinburgh EH14 ...... 33 C1
Edinburgh EH14 ...... 45 C4
Murrayburn Prim Sch
EH11 ...... 33 C2
Murrayburn Rd EH14 ...33 A2
Murray Cotts EH12 ...21 B2
Murrayfield Ave
EH12 ...... 23 C3
Murrayfield Dr EH12 ...23 B3
Murrayfield Gdns
EH12 ...... 23 C3
Murrayfield Hospl
EH12 ...... 22 C3
Murrayfield Pl EH12 ...23 C3
Murrayfield Rd EH12 ...23 B4
Murrayfield Rugby Gd
EH12 ...... 23 C3
Murrays Brae, The ...59 B4
Murrays, The ...59 B4

Mus of Childhood*
EH1 ...... 64 B3
Mus of Edinburgh*
EH1 ...... 64 B3
Mus of Fire* EH3 ...62 C2
Mus of Scotland*
EH1 ...... 64 A3
Musselburgh Burgh Prim
Sch EH21 ...... 31 B2
Musselburgh Gram Sch
EH21 ...... 31 B1
Musselburgh Rd
EH15 ...... 30 A3
Musselburgh Sta
EH21 ...... 42 C4
Myreside Ct EH10 ...36 B3
Myreside Rd EH10 ...36 B3
Myrtle Terr EH11 ...24 A1

N
Nantwich Dr EH7 ...18 A3
Napier Loan EH10 ...36 B4
Napier Rd
Edinburgh EH10 ...... 36 B4
Edinburgh, Sighthill
...... 24 B1
Napier Univ EH11 ...33 C2
Napier Univ (Craighouse
Campus) EH10 ...... 36 A2
Napier Univ
(Craiglockhart Campus)
EH14 ...... 35 C1
Napier Univ (Marchmont
Campus) EH9 ...... 25 C1
Napier Univ (Merchiston
Campus) EH10 ...... 36 C3
National Gallery of
Scotland* EH2 ...... 62 C3
National Liby of
Scotland* EH1 ...... 64 A3
National Mon* EH7 ...64 B4
National Portrait Gall*
EH2 ...... 64 A4
Neidpath Ct EH12 ...20 C3
Nellfield EH16 ...... 51 A4
Nelson St EH3 ...... 62 C4
Netherbank EH16 ...50 B2
Netherbank View
EH16 ...... 50 B2
Netherby Rd EH5 ...06 C2
Nether Craigour
EH17 ...... 39 C1
Nether Craigwell
EH8 ...... 64 C3
Nether Currie Cres
EH14 ...... 45 A1
Nether Currie Pl
EH14 ...... 45 A1
Nether Currie Prim Sch
EH14 ...... 45 A1
Nether Liberton Ct
EH16 ...... 38 C2
Newbattle Terr EH10 ...37 A4
New Bell's Ct EH6 ...08 C1
New Broompark EH5 ...06 A3
New Broughton 5
...... 15 C2
New Coll EH1 ...... 62 C3
Newcraighall Bsns Pk
EH15 ...... 41 A4
Newcraighall Dr
EH21 ...... 41 C4
Newcraighall Prim Sch
EH21 ...... 32 A4
Newcraighall Rd
EH15 ...... 41 B4
Newcraighall Sta
EH21 ...... 41 C4
New Cut Rigg EH6 ...07 C1
Newhailes Ave EH21 ...30 C2
Newhailes Cres ...30 B2
Newhailes Rd
Musselburgh EH21 ...30 C2
Newhailes Rd
Edinburgh EH15 ...... 30 A1
Edinburgh EH2 ...... 30 C1
Newhaven Heritage
Mus* EH6 ...... 7 C3
Newhaven Main St
EH6 ...... 07 B3
Newhaven Pl EH6 ...07 C3
Newhaven Rd EH6 ...07 C3
Newington Rd EH9 ...26 A1
New John's Pl EH8 ...65 B3
New La EH6 ...... 07 C2
New Lairdship Pl
EH11 ...... 33 C3
New Lairdship Yards
...... 33 C3
Newlands Pk EH9 ...38 B4
New Mart Rd EH14 ...35 A3
New Mkt L Village
EH14 ...... 35 B3
New Mkt Rd EH14 ...35 B3

New Orchardfield
EH6 ...... 16 B4
New Skinners Cl EH1 ...64 B3
New St Edinburgh EH1 ...64 B3
New Swanston EH10 ...48 B1
Newtoft St EH17 ...52 A1
Newton Church Rd
EH22 ...... 53 B3
Newton St EH11 ...24 A1
New Tower Pl EH15 ...19 A1
Nicholfield EH6 ...07 C2
Nicolson Sq EH8 ...65 B2
Nicolson St EH8 ...65 B2
Niddrie Farm Gr
EH16 ...... 40 A4
Niddrie Ho Ave 7
EH16 ...... 40 A3
Niddrie Ho Dr EH16 ...40 C3
Niddrie Ho Pk ...40 A3
Niddrie Mains Ct
EH16 ...... 40 C4
Niddrie Mains Dr
Edinburgh EH16 ...... 40 A4
Niddrie Mains Rd
EH16 ...... 40 C4
Niddrie Mains Terr
Edinburgh EH16 ...... 28 B1
Edinburgh EH16 ...... 40 A4
Niddrie Marischal
Crescent 4
EH16 ...... 40 B3
Niddrie Marischal Drive
5 EH16 ...... 40 B3
Niddrie Marischal
Gardens 3 EH16 ...40 B3
Niddrie Marischal Green
6 EH16 ...... 40 B3
Niddrie Marischal Grove
EH16 ...... 40 C4
Niddrie Marischal Loan
EH16 ...... 40 A3
Niddrie Marischal Place
EH16 ...... 40 B3
Niddrie Marischal Road
EH16 ...... 40 B3
Niddrie Marischal Street
2 ...... 40 A3
Niddrie Mill Ave
EH15 ...... 40 C4
Niddrie Mill Cres
EH15 ...... 28 C1
Niddrie Mill Dr EH15 ...40 C4
Niddrie Mill Gr EH15 ...40 C4
Niddrie Mill Gr EH15 ...40 C4
Niddrie Mill Prim Sch
EH15 ...... 40 C4
Niddrie Mill Terr
EH15 ...... 40 C4
Niddry St EH1 ...64 B3
Niddry St S EH1 ...64 B2
Nidrie Cotts EH15 ...41 B4
Nidrie Ho Gdns EH16 ...40 C3
Nidrie Ho Pk EH16 ...40 C3
Nidrie Ho Sq EH16 ...40 C3
Nigel Loan EH16 ...51 A4
Nile Gr EH10 ...37 A3
Noble Pl EH6 ...17 A4
North Bank St
Edinburgh EH1 ...... 62 C3
Edinburgh EH1 ...... 64 A3
North Bridge EH1 ...64 B3
North Bughtlin Bank
EH12 ...... 11 A1
North Bughtlin Brae
EH12 ...... 11 A1
North Bughtlinfield
EH12 ...... 10 C1
North Bughtlin Gate
EH12 ...... 11 A1
North Bughtlin Neuk
EH12 ...... 11 A1
North Bughtlin Pl
EH12 ...... 11 A1
North Bughtlin Rd
EH12 ...... 10 C1
Northbughtlinrig
EH12 ...... 10 C1
North Bughtlinside
EH12 ...... 10 C1
North Cairntow EH16 ...27 C1
North Castle St EH2 ...62 B4
North Charlotte St
EH2 ...... 62 B3
North Clyde St La
EH1 ...... 64 A4
Northcote St EH11 ...24 B2
North East Cir Pl 10
EH3 ...... 62 C4
North East Cumberland
St La EH3 ...... 15 B2
North East Thistle St La
EH2 ...... 62 C4
Northfield Ave EH8 ...28 A4
Northfield Broadway
Edinburgh EH8 ...... 17 C1
Edinburgh EH8 ...... 28 A4

Northfield Cir EH8 ...27 C4
Northfield Cres EH8 ...27 C4
Northfield Dr EH8 ...28 A3
Northfield Farm Ave
EH8 ...... 28 A3
Northfield Farm Rd
EH8 ...... 28 A3
Northfield Gdns EH8 ...28 A3
Northfield Gr EH8 ...28 A3
Northfield Pk EH8 ...28 A4
North Field Pk Gr ...28 A4
Northfield Rd EH8 ...27 C4
Northfield Sq EH8 ...28 A3
Northfield Terr EH8 ...27 C4
North Fort St ...08 A2
North Greens EH15 ...29 A1
North Gyle Ave EH12 ...21 A2
North Gyle Dr EH12 ...21 A3
North Gyle Farm Ct
...... 20 C2
North Gyle Farm La
EH12 ...... 20 C2
North Gyle Loan
EH12 ...... 20 C3
North Gyle Pk EH12 ...20 C3
North Gyle Rd EH12 ...21 A3
North Gyle Terr
...... 20 C2
North High St
Musselburgh EH21 ...31 A2
Musselburgh EH21 ...31 B2
North Hillhousefield
EH6 ...... 08 A3
North Junc St EH6 ...08 A2
Northlawn Ct EH4 ...12 A4
Northlawn Terr EH4 ...12 A4
North Leith Sands
EH6 ...... 08 A2
North Meggetland
EH14 ...... 36 B3
North Peffer Pl EH16 ...39 C4
North Pk Terr EH4 ...14 C2
North St Andrew La
EH2 ...... 64 A4
North St Andrew St
...... 64 A4
North St David St
Edinburgh EH2 ...... 62 C4
Edinburgh EH2 ...... 64 A4
Northumberland Pl La
EH3 ...... 15 B1
Northumberland St
EH3 ...... 15 B1
Northumberland St NE La
EH3 ...... 15 B1
Northumberland St Nw
La EH3 ...... 15 B1
Northumberland St Se La
EH3 ...... 15 B1
Northumberland St Sw La
EH3 ...... 15 B1
North Werber Pk
...... 14 A3
North Werber Pl EH4 ...14 A4
North West Circus Pl
...... 62 B4
North West Cumberland
St La EH3 ...... 15 A2
North West Thistle St La
EH2 ...... 62 C4
Norton Pk EH7 ...16 C2

O
Oakfield Pl EH8 ...65 B2
Oak La EH12 ...12 A1
Oaklands Specl Sch
...... 34 A3
Oakville Tr EH6 ...17 C4
Observatory Gn EH9 ...38 A2
Observatory Rd EH9 ...38 A2
Ocean Dr EH6 ...08 C2
Ocean Terminal Sh Ctr
...... 08 B3
Ochiltree Gdns EH16 ...39 B1
Ogilvie Terr EH11 ...36 A4
Old Broughton 4
...... 15 C2
Old Burdiehouse Rd
EH17 ...... 58 C3
Old Church La EH15 ...27 B2
Old Craighall Junc
EH21 ...... 43 A2
Old Craighall Rd
EH22 ...... 53 B2
Old Dalkeith Rd
Danderhall EH22 ...53 B2
Edinburgh EH16 ...39 B2
Edinburgh EH1 ...40 A1
Edinburgh EH1 ...52 A4
Old Farm Ave EH13 ...47 B3
Old Farm Pl EH13 ...47 B3
Old Fishmarket Cl
EH1 ...... 64 A3
Old Kirk Rd EH12 ...22 A3
Old Mill La EH16 ...38 C2
Old Tolbooth Wynd
EH8 ...... 64 B3

Olive Bank Rd EH21 ...31 A1
Orchard Bank EH4 ...14 A1
Orchard Brae EH4 ...14 B2
Orchard Brae Ave
...... 14 A1
Orchard Brae Gdns
EH4 ...... 14 B1
Orchard Brae Gdns W
...... 14 A1
Orchard Cres EH4 ...13 C1
Orchard Dr EH4 ...13 C1
Orchardfield Ave
...... 21 C2
Orchardhead Loan
EH16 ...... 50 C4
Orchardhead Rd
Edinburgh EH16 ...38 C1
Edinburgh EH16 ...50 C4
Orchard Pl EH4 ...14 A1
Orchard Rd EH4 ...14 A1
Orchard Rd S EH4 ...13 C1
Orchard Terr EH4 ...14 A1
Orchard Toll ...14 A1
Orchard View EH22 ...61 C2
Orch, The EH21 ...31 A1
Ormelie Terr EH15 ...29 B4
Ormidale Terr EH12 ...23 B3
Orrok Pk EH16 ...38 C2
Orwell Pl EH11 ...24 B2
Orwell Prim Sch
EH11 ...... 24 B2
Orwell Terr EH11 ...24 B2
Osborne Terr EH12 ...24 A3
Oswald Ct EH9 ...37 C3
Oswald Rd EH9 ...37 C3
Oswald Terr EH12 ...21 C2
Otterburn Pk EH14 ...47 A4
Our Dynamic Earth*
EH8 ...... 65 C4
Oxcraig St EH5 ...06 B3
Oxford St EH8 ...65 C1
Oxford Terr EH4 ...62 A4
Oxgangs Ave EH13 ...48 B3
Oxgangs Bank EH13 ...48 B2
Oxgangs Brae EH13 ...48 B2
Oxgangs Broadway
...... 48 A2
Oxgangs Cres EH13 ...48 B3
Oxgangs Dr EH13 ...48 B3
Oxgangs Farm Ave
EH13 ...... 48 A2
Oxgangs Farm Dr
...... 48 A2
Oxgangs Farm Gdns
...... 48 A2
Oxgangs Farm Gr
...... 48 A2
Oxgangs Farm Loan
...... 48 A2
Oxgangs Farm Terr
EH13 ...... 48 A3
Oxgangs Gdns EH13 ...48 A3
Oxgangs Gn EH13 ...48 B3
Oxgangs Gr EH13 ...48 B3
Oxgangs Hill EH13 ...48 B3
Oxgangs Ho EH13 ...48 B2
Oxgangs Loan EH13 ...48 B3
Oxgangs Medway
...... 48 B2
Oxgangs Path EH13 ...48 B2
Oxgangs Path E EH13 ...48 B2
Oxgangs Pk EH13 ...48 B2
Oxgangs Pl EH13 ...48 A3
Oxgangs Prim Sch
...... 48 A3
Oxgangs Rd EH10 ...48 C1
Oxgangs Rd N
Edinburgh EH13 ...... 47 C4
Edinburgh EH13 ...... 48 A3
Oxgangs Rise EH13 ...48 B3
Oxgangs Row EH13 ...48 B2
Oxgangs St EH13 ...48 B2
Oxgangs Terr EH13 ...48 B2
Oxgangs View EH13 ...48 B2

P
Paddockholm, The
EH12 ...... 22 A2
Paddock, The EH21 ...31 C3
Paisley Ave EH8 ...27 C3
Paisley Cres EH8 ...27 B4
Paisley Dr EH8 ...27 C3
Paisley Gdns EH8 ...27 C3
Paisley Gr EH8 ...27 C3
Paisley Terr EH8 ...27 B4
Palmer Rd EH14 ...44 B1
Palmerston Pl EH12 ...62 A3
Palmerston Pl La
...... 62 A3
Palmerston Rd EH9 ...25 C1
Pankmure Pl EH3 ...63 C1
Park Ave EH15 ...28 C3
Park Cres EH16 ...51 A4
Parker Ave EH7 ...18 A1
Parker Rd EH7 ...18 A1
Parker Terr EH7 ...18 B1

Park Gdns EH16 ...51 A4
Park Gr EH1 ...52 A2
Parkgrove Ave EH4 ...11 B2
Parkgrove Bank EH4 ...11 B2
Parkgrove Cres EH4 ...11 B2
Parkgrove Dr EH4 ...11 B2
Parkgrove Gdns EH4 ...11 B2
Parkgrove Gn EH4 ...11 B2
Parkgrove Loan EH4 ...11 B2
Parkgrove Neuk EH4 ...11 B2
Parkgrove Path EH4 ...11 B2
Parkgrove Pl EH4 ...11 B2
Parkgrove Rd EH4 ...11 B2
Parkgrove Row EH4 ...11 B2
Parkgrove St EH4 ...11 C2
Parkgrove Terr EH4 ...11 B2
Parkgrove View EH4 ...11 B2
Parkhead Ave EH11 ...34 A2
Parkhead Cres EH11 ...34 A2
Parkhead Dr EH11 ...34 B2
Parkhead Gdns EH11 ...34 A2
Parkhead Gr EH11 ...34 A2
Parkhead Loan EH11 ...34 B2
Parkhead Pl EH11 ...34 A2
Parkhead St EH11 ...34 A2
Parkhead Terr EH11 ...34 B3
Parkhead View EH11 ...34 A2
Park La EH15 ...28 C3
Park Pl EH6 ...07 B2
Park Rd EH6 ...07 B2
Parkside EH8 ...65 C1
Parkside Terr EH8 ...65 C1
Park Terr EH21 ...42 A4
Parkvale Pl EH6 ...17 A4
Park View EH21 ...41 C4
Parliament Sq EH6 ...08 B1
Parliament St EH6 ...08 B1
Parrotshot EH15 ...29 A1
Parsonage, The
...... 31 C2
Parsons Gn Prim Sch
...... 27 C3
Parsons Gn Terr 1
...... 17 B1
Patie's Rd EH14 ...47 B4
Patriothall 9 EH3 ...15 A2
Pattison St EH6 ...08 C1
Peacock Ct EH4 ...07 C3
Peacocktail Cl EH15 ...41 A4
Pearce Ave EH12 ...21 B3
Pearce Gr EH12 ...21 B3
Pearce Rd EH12 ...21 B3
Peatville Gdns EH14 ...34 C1
Peatville Terr EH14 ...34 C1
Peel Pentland Ctr
...... 58 C1
Peel Terr EH9 ...38 B4
Peffer Bank EH16 ...39 C4
Peffer Ind Est EH16 ...39 C4
Peffermill Ind Est
...... 39 B4
Peffermill Prim Sch
...... 39 C3
Peffermill Rd EH16 ...39 C4
Peffer Pl EH16 ...39 C4
Peffer St EH16 ...39 C4
Peggy's Mill Rd
...... 02 C1
Pembroke Pl EH12 ...24 A3
Pendreich Gr ...61 B1
Pennywell Ct EH4 ...05 A1
Pennywell Gdns EH4 ...05 A1
Pennywell Medway
...... 04 C1
Pennywell Pl EH4 ...05 A1
Pennywell Rd EH4 ...05 A1
Pennywell Villas EH4 ...05 A1
Pentland Ave EH13 ...47 A4
Pentland Cres EH10 ...48 C3
Pentland Dr EH10 ...48 B2
Pentland Gait Off Pk
...... 33 A1
Pentland Gr EH10 ...48 C3
Pentland Rd
Edinburgh EH13 ...... 46 C3
Edinburgh, Old Pentland
EH10 ...... 57 C1
Pentlands Gdns
EH10 ...... 48 C2
Pentland Terr EH10 ...48 C4
Peoples Story Mus The*
EH8 ...... 64 B3
Perdrixknowe ...35 C3
Perth St EH3 ...15 A2
Peveril Terr EH16 ...51 A4
Picardy Pl EH1 ...64 A4
Pier Pl EH6 ...07 B3
Piersfield Gr EH8 ...17 C1
Piersfield Pl EH8 ...17 C1
Piersfield Terr EH8 ...17 C1
Piershill La 7 EH8 ...17 B1
Piershill Pl 8 EH8 ...17 B1

Piershill Specl Sch
EH8 ....27 B4
Piershill Sq E EH8 ...17 C1
Piershill Sq W EH8 ...17 C1
Piershill Terr
🄳 Edinburgh EH8 ...17 C1
Edinburgh EH8 ....27 C4
Pilrig Gdns EH6 ....16 A3
Pilrig Ho Ct EH6 ...16 A4
Pilrig Ind Est EH6 ...16 A4
Pilrig Pk Specl Sch
EH6 ....16 A4
Pilrig St EH6 ......16 A3
Pilton Ave EH5 ....06 A1
Pilton Cres EH5 ...06 A1
Pilton Dr EH5 .....06 A1
Pilton Dr N EH5 ...06 A2
Pilton Gdns EH5 ...06 A1
Pilton Loan EH5 ...06 A1
Pilton Pk EH5 .....06 A1
Pilton Pl EH5 .....06 A1
Pinkhill EH12 ......22 B2
Pipe La EH15 ......18 C1
Pipe St EH15 ......18 C1
Pirig Cotts EH6 ....16 B3
Pirniefield Bank EH6 .17 B4
Pirniefield Gdns EH6 .17 B4
Pirniefield Gr EH6 ..17 B4
Pirniefield Pl EH6 ..17 B4
Pirniefield Terr EH6 .17 B4
Pirniehall Prim Sch
EH4 ....5 B1
Pirrie St EH6 ......16 B4
Pitlochry Pl 🄴 EH7 ..16 C2
Pitsligo Rd EH10 ...37 A4
Pitt St EH6 ....08 A1
Pittville St EH15 ...29 A4
Pittville St La EH15 .29 A4
Pleasance EH8 .....65 B2
Plewlands Ave EH10 .36 B2
Plewlands Gdns
EH10 ....36 B2
Plewlands Terr EH10 .36 B2
Pleydell Pl 🔟 EH16 ..51 A4
Pollard Glebe EH11 ..34 C4
Polton Rd EH18 ....60 C1
Polwarth Cres EH11 .24 C1
Polwarth Gdns EH11 .24 B1
Polwarth Gr
Edinburgh EH11 ...24 B1
Edinburgh EH11 ...36 B4
Polwarth Pk EH11 ..24 B1
Polwarth Pl EH11 ..24 B1
Polwarth Terr
Edinburgh EH11 ...24 B1
Edinburgh EH11 ...36 B4
Ponton St EH3 .....63 B1
Poplar La EH6 .....08 C1
Porteous Pend EH1 ..63 C2
Porterfield Rd EH4 ..14 A3
Portgower Pl EH4 ..14 C2
Port Hamilton EH3 ..63 B2
Portland Pl EH6 ...08 A2
Portland St EH6 ...08 A2
Portobello High Sch
EH15 ....28 B3
Portobello High St
Edinburgh EH15 ...18 C1
Edinburgh EH15 ...28 C4
Portobello L Ctr★
EH15 ....18 C1
Portobello Rd EH7,
EH8 ....18 A2
Portsburgh Sq EH1 ..63 C2
Potterrow EH8 .....65 A2
Pottery, The EH15 ..18 C1
Powderhall Brae
EH7 ....15 C4
Powderhall Rd EH7 ..15 C3
Prestonfield Ave
EH16 ....39 A4
Prestonfield Bank
EH16 ....38 C4
Prestonfield Cres
EH16 ....38 C4
Prestonfield Gdns
EH16 ....38 C4
Prestonfield Ho EH16 .39 C4
Prestonfield Prim Sch
EH16 ....39 A3
Prestonfield Rd
EH16 ....38 C4
Prestonfield Terr
EH16 ....38 C4
Preston St Prim Sch
EH8 ....65 C1
Priestfield Ave EH16 .39 A4
Priestfield Cres EH16 .39 A4
Priestfield Gdns
EH16 ....39 A4
Priestfield Gr EH16 ..39 A4
Priestfield Rd EH16 ..27 A1
Priestfield Rd N
EH16 ....26 C1

Primrose Bank Rd
EH5 ....07 A2
Primrose St EH6 ...16 C4
Primrose Terr EH11 ..24 A1
Prince Regent St
EH6 ....08 B2
Princess Mall Sh Ctr
EH1 ....64 A3
Princess Margaret Rose
Hospl (Orthopaedic)
EH10 ....49 B1
Princes St
Edinburgh EH2 ....62 C3
Edinburgh EH2 ....64 A3
Promenade
Edinburgh EH15 ...18 B3
Edinburgh EH15 ...29 B4
Musselburgh EH21 ..31 A3
Prospect Bank Cres
EH6 ....17 A4
Prospect Bank Gdns
EH6 ....17 A4
Prospect Bank Gr
EH6 ....17 A4
Prospect Bank Pl
EH6 ....17 A4
Prospect Bank Rd
EH6 ....17 A4
Prospect Bank Specl Sch
EH6 ....17 A4
Prospect Bank Terr
EH6 ....17 A4
Provost Haugh EH14 .45 B1

Q

Quality St EH4 .....12 B3
Quality St Junc EH4 .12 B3
Quality St La EH4 ..12 B3
Quarrybank EH14 ...45 B4
Quarrybank Cl EH14 .45 B4
Quarrybank Ct EH14 .45 B4
Quarrybank End
EH14 ....45 B4
Quarry Cl EH8 .....65 B3
Quarry Cotts EH15 ..41 A4
Quarryview EH14 ...45 B4
Quayside St EH6 ...08 B1
Queen Charlotte La
EH6 ....08 C1
Queen Charlotte St
EH6 ....08 C1
Queen Margaret Cl
EH10 ....49 C1
Queen Margaret Coll
EH12 ....21 C4
Queen Margaret Coll
(Leith Campus) EH6 .16 C4
Queen's Ave
Edinburgh EH4 ....13 A2
Edinburgh EH4 ....13 B2
Queen's Bay Cres
EH15 ....29 C3
Queen's Cres EH9 ..38 B4
Queen's Dr
Edinburgh EH15 ...27 B2
Edinburgh EH8 ....17 A1
Edinburgh EH8 ....64 C3
Edinburgh EH8 ....65 C2
Queen St
Edinburgh EH2 ....62 C4
Edinburgh EH2 ....64 A4
Queen St Gdns E
EH3 ....62 C4
Queen St Gdns W
EH3 ....62 C4
Queen's Wlk EH16 ..40 A4
Quilts, The EH6 ...08 B1
Quilts Wynd EH6 ..08 A1

R

Raeburn Mews EH4 ..14 C2
Raeburn Pl EH4 ....14 C2
Raeburn St EH4 ...14 C2
Rae's Ct EH16 .....50 C1
Ramsay Pl EH15 ...19 A1
Ramsay Gdn EH1 ...62 C3

Ramsey La EH1 ....62 C3
Randolph Cliff EH3 ..62 A3
Randolph Cres EH3 ..62 A3
Randolph La EH3 ..62 B3
Rankeillor St EH8 ..65 B1
Rankin Ave EH9 ...38 A2
Rankin Dr EH9 .....38 A2
Rankin Rd EH9 ....38 B3
Rannoch Gr EH4 ...11 C1
Rannoch Pl EH4 ...11 C1
Rannoch Rd EH4 ...11 C1
Rannoch Terr EH4 ..11 C1
Ransome Gdns EH4 ..11 C1
Ratcliffe Terr EH9 ..26 A1
Rathbone Pl EH15 ..19 A1
Ravelston Dykes
EH12 ....23 C4
Ravelston Dykes La
EH4 ....22 C4
Ravelston Dykes Rd
Edinburgh EH4 ....12 C1
Edinburgh EH4 ....13 A1
Edinburgh EH4 ....23 A4
Ravelston Gdn EH4 ..23 A4
Ravelston Ho Gr 🔟
EH4 ....13 B2
Ravelston Ho Load
EH4 ....13 B1
Ravelston Ho Pk
EH4 ....13 B1
Ravelston Ho Rd EH4 .13 B1
Ravelston Hts EH4 ..13 A1
Ravelston Pk EH4 ..23 A4
Ravelston Pl EH4 ..24 B4
Ravelston Rise EH4 ..23 A4
Ravelston Terr EH4 ..14 B1
Ravenscroft Gdns
EH16 ....39 B1
Ravenscroft Pl EH17 .51 C1
Ravenscroft St EH17 .52 A1
Ravenswood Ave
EH16 ....39 B1
Redbraes Gr EH7 ...15 C4
Redbraes Pl EH7 ...15 C4
Redcroft St EH22 ...52 C4
Redford Ave EH13 ..47 B2
Redford Bank EH13 ..47 B2
Redford Cres EH13 ..47 B2
Redford Dr EH13 ...47 A2
Redford Gdns EH13 ..47 C2
Redford Gr EH13 ...47 C3
Redford Loan EH13 ..47 B2
Redford Neuk EH13 ..47 B2
Redford Pl EH13 ...47 C3
Redford Rd EH13 ...47 C2
Redford Terr EH13 ..47 B2
Redford Wlk EH13 ..47 B2
Redgauntlet Terr
EH16 ....39 A1
Redhall Ave EH14 ..35 A2
Redhall Bank Rd
EH14 ....35 A2
Redhall Cres EH14 ..34 C2
Redhall Dr EH14 ...34 C2
Redhall Gdns EH14 ..34 C2
Redhall Gr EH14 ...34 C2
Redhall Ho Dr EH14 .35 A1
Redhall Pl EH14 ...34 C2
Redhall Rd EH14 ...34 C2
Redhall View EH14 ..35 A1
Redheughs Ave EH12 .32 C4
Redheughs Rigg
EH12 ....32 C4
Regent Pl EH7 ....16 C1
Regent Rd EH7, EH8 .64 B4
Regent St EH15 ...29 A4
Regent St La EH15 ..29 A4
Regent Terr EH7 ...64 C4
Regent Terr Mews
EH7 ....64 C4
Regis Ct EH4 .....11 A4
Register Pl EH1 ...64 A4
Reid's Cl EH8 .....64 C3
Reid Terr EH3 ....14 C2
Relugas Gdns EH9 ..38 A3
Relugas Pl EH9 ...38 A3
Relugas Rd EH9 ...38 A3
Rennie's Isle
Edinburgh EH6 ....08 C2
Edinburgh EH6 ....08 C2
Research Ave S EH14 .44 B4
Research Ave N
EH14 ....32 B1
Restalrig Ave EH7 ..17 C1
Restalrig Cir EH7 ...17 B3
Restalrig Cres EH7 ..17 B3
Restalrig Gdns EH7 ..17 A3
Restalrig Rd EH6,EH7 .17 A3
Restalrig Rd S EH7 ..17 B3
Restalrig Terr EH7 ..17 C4
Riccarton Ave EH14 ..44 C1
Riccarton Cres EH14 .44 C1
Riccarton Dr EH14 ..44 B1

Riccarton Gr EH14 ..44 C1
Riccarton Mains Rd
Currie EH14 ......32 B1
Currie EH14 ......44 C2
Richmond La EH8 ...65 B2
Richmond Pl EH8 ..65 B2
Richmond Terr EH11 .63 A2
Riding Pk EH4 ....11 A4
Riego St EH3 .....63 B2
Rillbank Cres EH9 ..25 C1
Rillbank Terr EH9 ...25 C1
Ringwood Pl EH16 ..51 A4
Rintoul Pl EH3 ....15 A2
Riselaw Cres EH10 ..48 C3
Riselaw Pl EH10 ...48 C4
Riselaw Rd EH10 ...48 C4
Riselaw Terr EH10 ..48 C4
Ritchie Pl EH11 ...24 B1
Riversdale Cres EH12 .23 B3
Riversdale Gr EH12 ..23 B3
Riversdale Rd EH12 ..23 B3
Riverside EH3 .....03 A3
Riverside Gdns EH31 .31 A1
Riverside Rd EH30 ..10 A3
R L Stevenson's
Birthplace & Mus★
EH3 ....15 B3
Robb's Loan EH14 ..35 B4
Robb's Loan Gr EH14 .35 B4
Robert Burns Dr
EH16 ....38 C1
Robertson Ave EH11 .23 C1
Robertson's Cl EH1 ..64 B2
Rocheid Pk EH4 ...14 A4
Rochester Terr EH10 .36 C4
Rodney Pl EH7 ....15 B2
Rodney St EH7 ....15 B3
Romero Pl EH16 ..26 B1
Rosebank Cotts EH3 ..63 A2
Rosebank Gdns EH5 ..06 C1
Rosebank Gr EH5 ...06 C1
Rosebank Rd EH5 ...06 C1
Rosebery Cres EH12 ..24 B3
Rosebery Cres La
EH12 ....24 B3
Edinburgh EH12 ...24 B3
Roseburn Ave EH12 ..23 C3
Roseburn Cliff EH12 ..23 C3
Roseburn Dr EH12 ..23 C3
Roseburn Gdns EH12 .23 C3
Roseburn Maltings
EH12 ....24 A3
Roseburn Pl EH12 ..23 C3
Roseburn Prim Sch
EH12 ....23 C2
Roseburn St EH12 ..23 C2
Roseburn Terr EH12 ..23 C2
Rose Ct EH4 ......12 A4
Rosefield Ave EH15 ..29 C4
Rosefield Ave La
EH15 ....28 C4
Rosefield La EH15 ..28 C4
Rosefield Pl EH15 ..28 C4
Rosefield St EH15 ..28 C4
Rosemount Bldgs
EH3 ....63 A2
Roseneath Pl
Edinburgh EH9 ....25 C1
Roseneath St EH9 ..25 C1
Roseneath Tr EH9 ..25 C1
Rose Pk EH5 ......07 A1
Rose St EH2 ......62 C3
Rose St North La
Edinburgh EH2 ...62 C3
Edinburgh EH2 ...64 A4
Rose St South La
Edinburgh EH2 ...62 C3
Edinburgh EH2 ...64 A4
Rosevale Pl EH6 ...17 A4
Rosevale Terr EH6 ..16 C4
Roseville Gdns EH5 ..07 B2
Ross Gdns EH9 ....38 B3
Rossie Pl
Edinburgh EH7 ...16 B2
Edinburgh EH7 ...16 C2
Rosslyn Cres EH6 ..16 A3
Rosslyn Terr EH6 ...16 A3
Ross Pl EH9 ......38 B3
Ross Rd EH16 .....38 C2
Rothesay Mews EH3 ..24 B4
Rothesay Pl
Edinburgh EH3 ...62 A3
Musselburgh EH21 ..31 C1
Rothesay Terr
EH3 ....24 B4
Roull Gr EH12 .....22 A1
Roull Pl EH12 .....22 A1
Roull Rd EH12 ....21 C1
Rowallan Ct EH12 ..20 C3
Roxburgh Pl EH8 ..65 B2
Roxburgh St EH8 ..65 B2
Royal Blind Sch The
EH16 ....38 B3
Royal Botanic Gdn★
EH3 ....15 A3

Royal Cir EH3 .....62 B4
Royal Coll of Physicians
EH2 ....62 C4
Royal Cres EH3 ...15 B2
Royal (Dick) Veterinary
Coll (EH) 65 B1
Royal Edinburgh Hospl
EH10 ....36 B3
Royal High Prim Sch The
EH8 ....27 C4
Royal High Sch The
EH4 ....11 C3
Royal Hospl for Sick
Children EH9 .....25 C1
Royal Infirmary of
Edinburgh
Edinburgh, Edmonstone
EH16 ....40 A1
Edinburgh, West
Meadow Park EH3 ..65 A2
Royal Mile Prim Sch
EH8 ....64 C3
Royal Mus★ EH1 ...65 A2
Royal Observatory★
EH9 ....37 C1
Royal Pk Terr EH8 ..17 A1
Royal Scottish Acad★
EH2 ....62 C3
Royal Terr EH7 ....64 C4
Royal Victoria Hospl
EH4 ....14 A2
Royal Yacht Britannia
(Former)★ EH6 ....8 B3
Royston Mains Ave
EH5 ....05 C2
Royston Mains Cl
EH5 ....06 A2
Royston Mains Cres
EH5 ....05 C2
Royston Mains Gdns
EH5 ....06 A2
Royston Mains Gn
EH5 ....06 A2
Royston Mains Pl
EH5 ....05 C2
Royston Mains Rd
EH5 ....06 A2
Royston Mains St
EH5 ....06 A2
Royston Prim Sch .6 A2
Royston Terr EH3 ..15 A4
Rudolf Steiner Sch
EH10 ....36 B4
Russell Gdns EH12 ..23 C3
Russell Rd EH11 ...24 A2
Russel Pl EH5 .....07 A2
Rutherford Dr EH16 ..39 A1
Ruthven Pl EH16 ..39 A1
Rutland Ct La EH3 ..63 B2
Rutland Sq 62 B2
Rutland St 62 B2
Ryehill Ave EH6 ...17 A4
Ryehill Gdns EH6 ..17 A4
Ryehill Gr EH6 ....17 A4
Ryehill Pl EH6 ....17 A4
Ryehill Terr EH6 ...17 A4

S

Saddletree Loan
EH16 ....39 B2
St Alban's Rd EH9 ..38 A3
St Andrew Pl EH6 ..16 C4
St Andrew Sq EH2 ..64 A4
St Anthony La EH6 ..08 B1
St Anthony Pl EH6 ..08 B1
St Anthony St EH6 ..08 B1
St Augustine's RC High
Sch EH12 ....33 B4
St Bernard's Cres
EH4 ....14 C1
St Bernard's Row 🄱
EH4 ....15 A2
St Catherine's Gdns
EH12 ....22 C2
St Catherine's Manor
EH12 ....22 C2
St Catherine's Pl EH9 .26 A1
St Catherine's RC Prim
Sch EH16 ....51 A1
St Clair Ave EH6 ...16 C3
St Clair Pl EH6 ....16 C3
St Clair Rd EH6 ...16 C3
St Clair St EH6 ....16 C3
St Clair Terr EH10 ..36 B2
St Colme St EH3 ...62 B4
St Colm's Ed Ctr & Coll
EH3 ....15 A3
St Crispin's Specl Sch
EH9 ....38 A3
St Cuthbert's RC Prim
Sch EH14 ....35 C4
St David's Pl EH3 ..63 A2
St David's RC Prim Sch
EH11 ....35 B2
St David's Terr EH3 ..63 A2
St Fillan's Terr EH10 .36 C2

St Francis's RC Prim Sch
EH16 ....40 A4
St George's Sch
EH12 ....24 A4
St Georges Sch for girls
EH12 ....23 C3
St Giles' St 64 A3
St James Ctr EH1 ..64 A4
St James Pl EH1 ...64 A4
St James Sq EH1 ..64 A4
St John's Ave EH12 ..22 A2
St John's Cres EH12 .22 A2
St John's Gdns EH12 .22 A2
St John's Hill 64 B2
St John's RC Prim Sch
EH15 ....28 C3
St John St EH8 ...64 B3
St John's Terr EH12 ..22 A2
St John Vianney RC Prim
Sch EH16 ....39 A1
St Joseph's Prim Sch
EH11 ....34 A3
St Katharine's Brae
EH16 ....50 C2
St Katharine's Cres
EH16 ....50 C2
St Katharine's Loan
EH16 ....51 A1
St Leonard's Bank
EH8 ....65 C1
St Leonard's Crag
EH8 ....65 C1
St Leonard's Hill EH8 .65 B1
St Leonard's La EH8 ..65 B1
St Leonard's St EH8 ..65 B1
St Margaret's Pl EH9 .37 B4
St Margaret's Prim Sch
EH20 ....59 B1
St Margaret's Rd
EH9 ....37 A4
St Margaret's Sch
EH16 ....39 C3
St Mark's La EH15 ..29 A4
St Mark's Pl EH15 ..29 A4
St Mark's RC Prim Sch
EH14 ....44 A3
St Mary's (Leith) RC Prim
Sch EH6 ....9 A1
St Mary's Music Sch
EH12 ....24 A4
St Mary's Pl EH15 ..29 B3
St Mary's Pl La EH15 .29 B4
St Mary's RC Cath★
EH1 ....64 A4
St Mary's RC Prim Sch
EH1 ....15 C2
St Mary's St EH1 ..64 B3
St Michael's Ave
EH21 ....31 B1
St Nicholas (Specl Sch)
EH11 ....23 C2
St Ninian's Dr EH12 ..21 C3
St Ninian's RC Prim Sch
EH7 ....17 B2
St Ninian's Rd EH12 ..21 C3
St Ninians Row EH1 ..64 B4
St Ninian's Terr EH10 .36 B2
St Patrick Sq EH8 ..65 B1
St Patrick St EH8 ..65 B1
St Peter's Bldgs
EH3 ....63 A1
St Peter's Pl EH3 ..63 A1
St Peter's RC Prim Sch
EH10 ....37 A3
St Ronan's Terr EH10 .36 C2
St Serf's Sch EH12 ..23 A3
St Stephen Pl EH3 ..15 A2
St Stephen St EH3 ..15 A2
St Teresa Pl EH3 ..36 B4
St Thomas of Aquin's
High Sch EH3 ....63 B1
St Thomas Rd EH9 ..37 C3
St Triduana's Chapel★
EH7 ....17 B2
St Vincent St EH3 ..15 A2
Salamander Pl EH6 ..09 A1
Salamander St EH6 ..09 A1
Salamander Yds EH6 .09 A1
Salisbury Pl EH9 ..26 A1
Salisbury Rd EH16 ..26 B1
Salmond Pl 🄱 EH7 ..16 C2
Salter's Rd EH22 ...55 C2
Salvesen Cres EH4 ..05 A2
Salvesen Gdns EH4 ..05 A2
Salvesen Gr EH4 ...05 A2
Salvesen Terr EH4 ..05 A2
Sand Port EH6 ....08 C2
Sandport Pl EH6 ...08 B2
Sandport St EH6 ...08 B2
Sand Port Trad Est
EH6 ....8 B2
Sauchiebank EH11 ..24 A2
Saughton Ave
Edinburgh EH11 ...23 B1
Edinburgh EH11 ...35 B4
Saughton Cres EH12 .23 A2

Saughton Gdns EH12 ...23 A2
Saughton Gr EH12 ...23 A2
Saughtonhall Ave EH12 ...23 A2
Saughtonhall Ave W EH12 ...23 A2
Saughtonhall Cir EH12 ...23 B2
Saughtonhall Cres EH12 ...23 A2
Saughtonhall Dr EH12 ...23 A2
Saughtonhall Gdns EH12 ...23 B2
Saughtonhall Gr EH12 ...23 B2
Saughtonhall Pl EH12 ...23 B2
Saughtonhall Terr EH12 ...23 B2
Saughton Loan EH12 ...23 A2
Saughton Mains Ave EH11 ...34 B4
Saughton Mains Dr EH11 ...34 B3
Saughton Mains Gdns EH11 ...34 B3
Saughton Mains Gr EH11 ...34 C3
Saughton Mains Loan EH11 ...34 B3
Saughton Mains Pk EH11 ...34 B4
Saughton Mains Pl EH11 ...34 B4
Saughton Mains St EH11 ...34 C4
Saughton Pk EH12 ...23 A2
Saughton Rd EH11 ...34 B4
Saughton Rd N EH12 ...22 A1
Savile Pl EH9 ...38 B3
Savile Terr EH9 ...38 B3
Saxe Coburg Pl EH3 ...15 A2
Saxe Coburg St EH3 ...15 A2
School Brae
  Bonnyrigg and Lasswade EH18 ...60 C1
  Edinburgh EH4 ...03 A2
School Gn EH18 ...60 C1
Sciennes EH9 ...26 A1
Sciennes Gdns EH9 ...26 A1
Sciennes Hill Pl 4 EH9 ...26 A1
Sciennes Ho Pl 3 EH9 ...26 A1
Sciennes Pl 4 EH9 ...26 A1
Sciennes Prim Sch EH9 ...25 C1
Sciennes Rd EH9 ...25 C1
Scone Gdns EH8 ...17 B1
Scotch Whisky Heritage Ctr The★ EH1 ...62 C2
Scotland St EH3 ...15 B2
Scottish Ag Agency EH12 ...20 C4
Scottish Nat Gall of Mod Art★ EH4 ...24 A4
Scottish Parliament★ EH8 ...64 C3
Scott Mon★ EH2 ...64 A3
Seacot EH6 ...17 B4
Seafield Ave EH6 ...17 B4
Seafield Moor Rd ...57 B1
Seafield Pl EH6 ...17 B4
Seafield Rd EH6 ...17 C4
Seafield Rd E EH15 ...18 A3
Seafield St EH6 ...17 C4
Seafield Way EH15 ...18 A3
Seaforth Dr EH4 ...13 B2
Seaforth Terr 4 EH4 ...13 B2
Sealcar St EH5 ...06 A3
Seaport St EH6 ...08 C1
Seaview Cres EH15 ...29 C3
Seaview Terr EH15 ...30 A3
Second Gait EH14 ...44 A4
Semple St EH3 ...63 B2
Seton Pl EH9 ...26 A1
Sghtn Mns Bnk EH11 ...34 C4
Shaftesbury Pk EH11 ...36 A4
Shandon Cres EH11 ...36 A4
Shandon Pl EH11 ...36 A4
Shandon Rd EH11 ...36 A4
Shandon St EH11 ...36 A4
Shandon Terr EH11 ...36 A4
Shandwick Pl EH2 ...62 A3
Shanter Way 7 EH14 ...38 C1
Sharpdale Loan EH16 ...39 A3
Shaw's Pl EH7 ...16 A3
Shaw's Sq
  Edinburgh EH1 ...15 C2
  Edinburgh EH1 ...16 A2
Shaw's St EH7 ...16 A3
Shaw's Terr EH7 ...16 A3

Sheriff Bank EH6 ...08 B1
Sheriff Brae EH6 ...08 B1
Sheriffhall Junc EH22 ...53 C1
Sheriff Pk EH6 ...08 B1
Shore Edinburgh EH6 ...08 B1
  Edinburgh EH6 ...08 C2
Shore Pl EH6 ...08 C2
Shorthope St EH21 ...31 B2
Shrub Mount EH15 ...18 C1
Shrub Pl La EH7 ...16 A3
Sienna Gdns EH9 ...26 A1
Sighthill Ave EH11 ...34 A2
Sighthill Bank EH11 ...33 C2
Sighthill Cres EH11 ...33 C1
Sighthill Ct EH11 ...33 C2
Sighthill Dr EH11 ...33 C1
Sighthill Gdns EH11 ...33 C1
Sighthill Gn EH11 ...33 C2
Sighthill Gr EH11 ...34 A2
Sighthill Ind Est EH11 ...33 A3
Sighthill Loan EH11 ...33 C2
Sighthill Neuk EH11 ...33 C2
Sighthill Pk EH11 ...33 C2
Sighthill Prim Sch EH11 ...33 C1
Sighthill Rd EH11 ...33 C1
Sighthill Rise EH11 ...33 C1
Sighthill St EH11 ...33 C1
Sighthill Terr EH11 ...33 C2
Sighthill View EH11 ...33 C1
Sighthill Wynd EH11 ...33 C2
Silverknowes Loan ...12 B4
Silverknowes Ave EH4 ...12 B4
Silverknowes Bank EH4 ...12 B4
Silverknowes Brae
  Edinburgh EH4 ...12 B4
  Edinburgh EH4 ...12 C4
Silverknowes Cres EH4 ...12 B4
Silverknowes Ct EH4 ...12 B4
Silverknowes Dell EH4 ...12 B4
Silverknowes Dr EH4 ...12 B4
Silverknowes Eastway
  EH12 ...12 C4
  Edinburgh EH4 ...12 C4
Silverknowes Gdns EH4 ...04 B1
Silverknowes Gn EH4 ...12 C4
Silverknowes Gr EH4 ...04 B1
Silverknowes Hill EH4 ...12 C4
Silverknowes Midway EH4 ...12 C4
Silverknowes Neuk EH4 ...12 C4
Silverknowes Parkway EH4 ...04 B1
Silverknowes Pl EH4 ...04 B1
Silverknowes Prim Sch EH4 ...4 C1
Silverknowes Rd
  Edinburgh EH4 ...04 A2
  Edinburgh EH4 ...12 B4
Silverknowes Rd E EH4 ...12 C4
Silverknowes Rd S EH4 ...12 C4
Silverknowes Southway EH4 ...12 C4
Silverknowes Terr EH4 ...12 C4
Silverknowes View ...12 C4
Simon Sq EH8 ...65 B2
Sinclair Cl EH11 ...24 A1
Sinclair Gdns EH11 ...24 A1
Sinclair Pl EH11 ...23 C1
Sir Harry Lauder Rd
  Edinburgh EH15 ...18 B1
  Edinburgh EH15 ...28 C4
Sir William Fraser Homes EH13 ...46 C3
Slateford Gn EH14 ...35 C4
Slateford Rd EH14 ...35 C4
Slateford Sta EH14 ...35 B4
Sleigh Dr EH7 ...17 B2
Sleigh Gdns EH7 ...17 B2
Sloan St EH6 ...16 B3
Smeaton Gr EH21 ...43 C3
Smithfield St EH11 ...23 C1
Smith's Pl EH6 ...16 B4
Smithy Gn Ave EH22 ...53 A3
Somerset Pl EH6 ...16 C4
Southbank EH4 ...12 A4
Southbank Ct EH4 ...12 A4
South Barnton Ave EH4 ...12 A4
South Beechwood EH12 ...22 C2

South Bridge EH1 ...64 A3
South Charlotte St EH2 ...62 B3
South Clerk St EH8 ...65 B1
South College St ...65 A2
South East Circus Pl ...62 B4
South East Cumberland St La EH3 ...62 B4
South East Thistle St La EH2 ...62 C4
South Elixa Pl EH8 ...27 C4
South Ettrick Rd EH10 ...36 B4
Southfield Bank EH15 ...28 B2
Southfield Farm Gr EH15 ...28 A3
Southfield Gdns E EH15 ...28 B3
Southfield Gdns W EH15 ...28 B3
Southfield Load EH15 ...28 B2
Southfield Loan EH15 ...28 B2
Southfield Pl EH15 ...28 C4
Southfield Rd E EH15 ...28 A3
Southfield Rd W EH15 ...28 A2
Southfield Sq EH15 ...28 B2
Southfield Terr EH15 ...28 B2
South Fort St EH6 ...08 A1
Son Gayfield La 8 EH1 ...16 A2
South Gillsland Rd EH10 ...36 B3
South Gray's Cl EH1 ...64 B3
South Gray St EH9 ...26 B1
South Groathill Ave EH4 ...13 B2
South Gyle Access EH12 ...33 B4
South Gyle Broadway
  Edinburgh EH12 ...20 B1
  Edinburgh EH12 ...33 B4
South Gyle Cres
  Edinburgh EH12 ...33 A4
  Edinburgh EH12 ...33 A4
South Gyle Cres La EH12 ...33 A4
South Gyle Gdns EH12 ...21 A1
South Gyle Ind Est EH12 ...33 A4
South Gyle Loan EH12 ...21 A1
South Gyle Mains EH12 ...21 A1
South Gyle Pk
  Edinburgh EH12 ...21 A1
  Edinburgh EH12 ...33 A4
South Gyle Rd EH12 ...21 A1
South Gyle Sta EH12 ...21 A1
South Gyle Wynd EH12 ...33 A4
Southhouse Ave EH17 ...51 A1
Southhouse Broadway EH17 ...59 A4
Southhouse Cres EH17 ...59 A4
Southhouse Gdns EH17 ...59 A4
Southhouse Gr EH17 ...59 A4
Southhouse Loan EH17 ...51 A1
Southhouse Medway EH17 ...51 A1
Southhouse Rd
  Edinburgh EH17 ...51 A1
  Edinburgh EH17 ...51 A1
Southhouse Sq EH17 ...51 A1
Southhouse Terr EH17 ...51 A1
South Lauder Rd EH9 ...38 A4
South Laverockbank Ave EH5 ...07 B2
Southlawn Ct EH4 ...12 A4
South Learmonth Gd EH4 ...62 A4
South Lorne Pl 4 EH6 ...16 B3
South Maybury EH12 ...20 C2
South Mellis Pk EH8 ...28 A4
South Morningside Prim Sch EH10 ...36 C2
South Morton St EH15 ...29 B3
South Oswald Rd EH9 ...37 C3
South Oxford St EH8 ...26 B1
South Parrotshot EH15 ...29 A1
South Pk EH6 ...07 B2
South Sloan St EH6 ...16 B3
South St EH21 ...31 A2

South St Andrew St EH2 ...64 A4
South St David St EH2 ...64 A4
South Steil EH10 ...36 A1
South Trinity Rd EH5 ...07 A1
South West Cumberland St La EH3 ...15 B2
South West Thistle St La EH2 ...62 C4
Spa Pl EH15 ...19 A1
Speedwell Ave EH22 ...52 C4
Spencer Pl EH5 ...07 A2
Spence St EH16 ...26 B1
Spey St EH7 ...16 A3
Spey St La EH7 ...16 A3
Spey Terr EH7 ...16 A3
Spier's Pl EH6 ...08 B1
Spinney, The EH17 ...51 C2
Spittal St EH3 ...63 B2
Spottiswoode Rd EH9 ...25 B1
Spottiswoode St EH9 ...25 B1
Springfield EH6 ...16 B4
Springfield St EH6 ...16 C1
Spring Gdns EH8 ...16 C1
Springvalley Gdns EH10 ...36 C3
Springvalley Terr EH10 ...36 C3
Springwell Pl EH11 ...24 B2
Springwood Pk EH16 ...51 A4
Spylaw Ave EH13 ...46 B3
Spylaw Bank Rd EH13 ...46 C3
Spylaw Pk EH13 ...46 B3
Spylaw Rd EH10 ...36 B4
Spylaw St EH13 ...46 B3
Square, The EH22 ...53 A4
Stable La EH10 ...36 C3
Stafford St EH3 ...62 A3
Stair Pk EH12 ...22 C2
Stanedykehead EH16 ...50 B2
Stanhope Pl EH12 ...24 A3
Stanhope St EH12 ...24 A3
Stanley Pl EH7 ...16 C1
Stanley Rd EH6 ...07 B2
Stanley St EH15 ...28 C3
Stanwell St EH6 ...16 A4
Stapeley Ave EH7 ...18 A2
Starbank Rd EH5 ...07 B2
Station Brae EH15 ...28 C4
Station Rd
  Edinburgh EH12 ...22 A2
  Musselburgh EH21 ...31 B1
Stead's Pl EH6 ...16 B4
Steel's Pl EH10 ...37 A3
Steils, The EH10 ...36 A1
Stenhouse Ave EH11 ...34 C4
Stenhouse Ave W EH11 ...34 C4
Stenhouse Cotts EH11 ...34 C4
Stenhouse Cres EH11 ...34 C4
Stenhouse Cross EH11 ...34 C4
Stenhouse Dr
  Edinburgh EH11 ...34 B4
  Edinburgh EH11 ...34 C4
Stenhouse Gdns EH11 ...34 C4
Stenhouse Gdns N EH11 ...34 C4
Stenhouse Gr EH11 ...34 C4
Stenhouse Mill Cres EH11 ...35 A3
Stenhouse Mill La EH11 ...35 A3
Stenhouse Mill Wynd EH11 ...35 A3
Stenhouse Pl E EH11 ...34 C4
Stenhouse Pl W EH11 ...34 C4
Stenhouse Prim Sch EH11 ...34 B4
Stenhouse Rd EH11 ...34 B4
Stenhouse St E EH11 ...34 C4
Stenhouse St W
  Edinburgh EH11 ...34 B4
  Edinburgh EH11 ...34 C4
Stennis Gdns EH17 ...51 B3
Stevenla's Cl EH1 ...64 A3
Stevenson Ave EH11 ...23 B1
Stevenson Coll EH11 ...33 B3
Stevenson Dr EH11 ...35 A4
Stevenson Gr EH11 ...23 B1
Stevenson Rd EH11 ...23 B1
Stevenson Terr EH11 ...23 B1
Stewartfield EH6 ...15 C4
Stewart Gr EH22 ...52 C4
Stewart's Melville Coll EH4 ...14 A1
Stewart Terr
  Edinburgh EH11 ...23 C1

Stewart Terr continued
  Edinburgh EH11 ...36 A4
Stirling Rd EH5 ...07 A2
Stockbridge Prim Sch EH3 ...15 A2
Stoneybank Ave EH21 ...42 C4
Stoneybank Cres EH21 ...43 A4
Stoneybank Ct EH21 ...30 C1
Stoneybank Dr EH21 ...30 C1
Stoneybank Gdns EH21 ...30 C1
Stoneybank Gdns N EH21 ...30 C1
Stoneybank Gdns S EH21 ...43 A4
Stoneybank Gr EH21 ...43 A4
Stoneybank Pl EH21 ...43 A4
Stoneybank Rd EH21 ...43 A4
Stoneybank Terr EH21 ...43 A4
Stoneyhill Ave EH21 ...30 C1
Stoneyhill Cres EH21 ...30 C1
Stoneyhill Ct EH21 ...30 C1
Stoneyhill Dr EH21 ...30 C1
Stoneyhill Farm Rd EH21 ...31 A1
Stoneyhill Gr EH21 ...30 C1
Stoneyhill Pl EH21 ...30 C1
Stoneyhill Prim Sch EH21 ...30 C1
Stoneyhill Rd EH21 ...30 C1
Stoneyhill Rise EH21 ...30 C1
Stoneyhill Steadings EH21 ...30 C1
Stoneyhill Terr EH21 ...30 C1
Stoneyhill Wynd 1 EH21 ...30 C1
Strachan Gdns EH4 ...12 C2
Strachan Rd EH4 ...12 C2
Straiton Mains EH20 ...58 C1
Straiton Pk EH20 ...58 C1
Straiton Pl EH15 ...29 A4
Straiton Rd EH20 ...58 C1
Strath Almond Gn EH4 ...10 B3
Strathalmond Pk EH4 ...10 B2
Strathalmond Rd EH4 ...10 B2
Strathearn Pl EH9 ...37 A4
Strathearn Rd EH9 ...37 B4
Strathfillan Rd EH9 ...37 B4
Stuart Cres EH12 ...21 A4
Stuart Gn EH12 ...21 A4
Stuart Pk EH12 ...21 A4
Stuart Sq EH12 ...21 A4
Stuart Wynd EH12 ...21 A4
Succoth Ave EH12 ...23 C4
Succoth Ct EH12 ...23 C4
Succoth Gdns EH12 ...23 C4
Succoth Pk EH12 ...23 C4
Succoth Pl EH12 ...23 C4
Suffolk Rd EH16 ...38 B3
Sugarhouse Cl EH8 ...64 B3
Summer Bank EH3 ...15 B2
Summerfield Gdns EH6 ...17 A4
Summerfield Pl EH6 ...17 A4
Summerhall EH8 ...65 B1
Summerhall Cres EH9 ...65 B1
Summerhall Pl EH9 ...65 B1
Summerhall Sq EH9 ...65 B1
Summerside Pl EH6 ...07 C2
Summerside St EH6 ...07 C1
Summertrees Ct EH16 ...39 A1
Sunbury Mews EH4 ...24 B4
Sunbury Pl EH4 ...24 B4
Sunbury St EH4 ...24 B4
Sunnybank Terr 8 EH7 ...17 A1
Sunny Side EH6 ...16 C2
Sutherland St EH12 ...24 A3
Swanfield EH6 ...08 B1
Swan Spring Ave EH10 ...48 C3
Swanston Ave EH10 ...48 C3
Swanston Cres EH10 ...48 C3
Swanston Dr EH10 ...57 A4
Swanston Gdns EH10 ...48 C1
Swanston Gn EH10 ...48 C1
Swanston Gr EH10 ...57 A4
Swanston Loan EH10 ...48 C1
Swanston Muir EH10 ...48 B1
Swanston Pl EH10 ...48 C1
Swanston Rd EH10 ...48 B1
Swanston Row EH10 ...48 C1
Swanston Terr EH10 ...49 A1
Swanston View EH10 ...48 C1
Swanston Way EH10 ...48 C1

Sycamore Gdns EH22 ...22 A2
Sydney Pk EH7 ...18 A2
Sydney Pl EH7 ...18 A2
Sydney Terr EH7 ...18 A2
Sylvan Pl EH9 ...25 C1
Syme Pl EH10 ...48 A4
Syme Rigg EH10 ...48 A4

T

Talisman Pl EH9 ...39 A1
Tantallon Pl EH9 ...25 C1
Tarvit St EH3 ...63 B1
Taylor Gdns EH6 ...08 B1
Taylor Pl 12 EH8 ...16 C1
Tay St EH11 ...24 B1
Telferton EH7 ...18 A1
Telford Coll (North Campus) EH5 ...6 A1
Telford Coll (South Campus) EH4 ...14 A4
Telford Dr EH4 ...13 C3
Telford Pl EH4 ...13 C3
Telford Rd EH4 ...13 C3
Templar's Crammond ...10 C4
Templeland Gr EH12 ...21 C3
Templeland Rd EH12 ...21 B3
Temple Pk Cres EH11 ...24 B1
Tennant St EH6 ...16 B4
Terrars Croft EH8 ...65 C1
Teviotdale Pl EH3 ...15 A2
Teviot Pl EH1 ...65 A2
Third Gait EH14 ...44 A3
Thirlestane La EH9 ...37 B4
Thirlestane Rd EH9 ...37 B4
Thistle Pl EH11 ...63 A1
Thistle St EH2 ...62 C4
Thomson Cres EH14 ...45 A1
Thomson Dr EH14 ...45 A1
Thomson Gr EH14 ...45 A1
Thomson Rd EH14 ...45 A1
Thorburn Gr EH13 ...47 B2
Thorburn Rd EH13 ...47 A2
Thorntreeside Ind Est EH6 ...16 C3
Thorntree St EH6 ...16 B4
Thornville Terr EH6 ...16 C3
Thornybauk
  Edinburgh EH3 ...63 B1
  Edinburgh EH3 ...63 B2
Timber Bush EH6 ...08 C2
Tinto Pl EH6 ...16 A4
Tipperlinn Rd EH10 ...36 C2
Tolbooth Wynd EH6 ...08 B1
Tollcross EH3 ...63 B1
Tollcross Prim Sch EH3 ...63 B1
Torphichen Pl EH3 ...63 A2
Torphichen St EH3 ...63 A2
Torphin Bank EH13 ...46 B1
Torphin Rd EH13 ...46 B1
Torrance Pk EH4 ...11 B1
Toward Ct EH12 ...20 C3
Towerbank Prim Sch EH15 ...19 A1
Tower Pl EH6 ...08 C2
Tower St EH6 ...08 C2
Trafalgar La EH6 ...07 C1
Trafalgar St EH6 ...08 A1
Traquair Pk E EH12 ...22 B2
Traquair Pk W EH12 ...22 A2
Traverse Theatre★ EH1 ...63 B2
Trench Knowe EH10 ...48 C1
Tressilian Gdns 8 EH16 ...39 A1
Trinity Acad EH6 ...7 B2
Trinity Cres EH5 ...07 A2
Trinity Ct EH5 ...06 C1
Trinity Gr EH5 ...07 A2
Trinity Mains EH5 ...07 A2
Trinity Prim Sch EH6 ...7 C2
Trinity Rd EH5 ...07 A1
Trinity Way EH5 ...07 A1
Tron Sq EH1 ...64 A3
Trotter Haugh EH9 ...37 C3
Turner Pk EH13 ...46 B1
Turnhouse Rd ...20 A4
Tweeddale Ct EH4 ...64 B3
Tyler's Acre Ave EH12 ...22 A1
Tyler's Acre Gdns EH12 ...22 A1
Tyler's Acre Rd EH12 ...22 A1
Tynecastle High Sch EH11 ...24 A1
Tynecastle La EH11 ...24 A1

Tynecastle Pk (Heart of
Midlothian FC)
EH11 ....24 A2
Tynecastle Terr
EH11 ....24 A1
Tytler Gdns
Edinburgh EH8 ....16 C1
Edinburgh EH8 ....64 C4

U

Ulster Cres EH8 ....27 C4
Ulster Dr EH8 ....27 C4
Ulster Gdns EH8 ......27 C3
Ulster Gr EH8 ....27 C3
Ulster Terr EH8 ......27 C3
Union Pl EH1 ....64 B4
Union St EH1 ....16 A2
Univ of Edinburgh
EH8 ....65 A2
Univ of Edinburgh (King's
Buildings Campus)
EH9 ....38 B2
Upper Bow EH1 ....64 A3
Upper Coltbridge Terr
EH12 ....23 C4
Upper Craigour
Edinburgh EH17 ......39 C1
Edinburgh EH17 ......52 A4
Upper Craigour Way
EH17 ....39 C1
Upper Cramond Ct
EH4 ....11 A4
Upper Dean Terr
EH4 ....62 A4
Upper Gilmore Pl
EH3 ....63 B1
Upper Gilmore Terr
EH3 ....63 B1
Upper Gray St EH9 ...26 A1
Upper Gr Pl EH3 ......63 A1
Upper Hermitage
EH6 ....16 C4
Usher H* EH1 ....63 B2

V

Valleyfield St EH3 ....63 B1
Vandeleur Ave EH7 ...18 A2
Vandeleur Gr EH7 ....18 B1
Vandeleur Pl EH7 ....18 B2
Veitch's Sq B EH4 ...15 A2
Ventnor Pl EH9 ....38 C4
Ventnor Terr EH9 .....38 B4
Vexhim Pk EH15 ......29 A1
Victoria Prim Sch EH6 .7 C3
Victoria St EH1 ......64 A2
Victoria Terr 64 A2
Victor Pk Terr EH12 ..21 C3
Viewcraig Gdns EH8 ..65 B2
Viewcraig St EH8 .....64 B3
Viewfield Ave 61 B1
Viewfield Rd EH14 ....46 A3
Viewforth
Edinburgh EH10 ......24 C1
Edinburgh EH11 ......63 A1
Viewforth Gdns EH10 .25 A1
Viewforth Sq EH10 ...24 C1
Viewforth Terr EH10 ..24 C1
Violet Terr EH11 .....24 A1
Vivian Terr EH4 ......12 C3

W

Wadingburn La EH18 ..60 B1
Wakefield Ave EH7 ...18 B2
Walker Cres EH22 ....61 C1
Walkers Ct EH14 .....34 A1

Walkers Rig EH14 ....34 A1
Walker St EH3 ....62 A3
Walkers Wynd EH14 ..34 A1
Walker Terr EH11 ....63 A2
Walter Scott Ave
EH16 ....39 A1
Wanless Ct EH21 .....31 C2
Wardie Ave EH5 ......06 C1
Wardieburn Dr EH5 ..06 B2
Wardieburn Pl E EH5 .06 B2
Wardieburn Pl N EH5 .06 B2
Wardieburn Pl S EH5 .06 B2
Wardieburn Pl W
EH5 ....06 A2
Wardieburn Rd EH5 ..06 A2
Wardieburn St E EH5 .06 B2
Wardieburn St W
EH5 ....06 A2
Wardieburn Terr
EH5 ....06 A2
Wardie Cres EH5 .....06 C2
Wardie Dell EH5 .....06 C2
Wardiefield EH5 ......06 B2
Wardie Gr EH5 ....06 B2
Wardie Ho La EH5 ....06 C2
Wardie Pk EH5 ....06 C1
Wardie Prim Sch EH5 .6 C2
Wardie Rd EH5 ....06 C2
Wardie Sq EH5 ....06 C2
Wardlaw Pl EH11 .....24 A1
Wardlaw St EH11 .....24 A1
Wardlaw Terr EH11 ...24 A1
Warrender Pk Cres
EH9 ....25 A1
Warrender Pk Rd
EH9 ....25 B1
Warrender Pk Terr
Edinburgh EH9 ....25 B1
Edinburgh EH9 ....63 C1
Warriston Ave EH3 ...15 B4
Warriston Cres EH3 ..15 B3
Warriston Dr EH3 ....15 A4
Warriston Gdns EH3 ..15 A4
Warriston Gr EH3 ....15 A4
Warriston Rd EH3,
EH7 ....15 A4
Warriston Terr EH3 ..15 A4
Washington La EH11 ..24 B2
Waterloo Pl EH1 .....64 A4
Water Of Leith Visitor
Ctr* EH14 ....35 B2
Waters' Cl EH1 ....08 C1
Water St EH6 ....08 C1
Watertoun Rd EH9 ...38 A3
Watson Cres EH11 ...24 B1
Watt's Cl EH21 ....31 A2
Wauchope Ave EH16 ..40 A4
Wauchope Cres
EH16 ....40 A4
Wauchope Pl EH16 ...40 A4
Wauchope Rd 40 A4
Wauchope Sq 40 A4
Wauchope Terr EH16 .40 A4
Waverley Bridge EH1 .64 A3
Waverley Pk EH8 .....16 C1
Waverley Pk Terr
EH8 ....16 C1
Waverley Pl EH7 .....16 C1
Waverley Sta EH1 ....64 A3
Waverley Steps EH2 ..64 A3
Weaver's Knowe Cres
EH14 ....44 B1
Wedderburn Terr
EH21 ....43 C3
Wee Brae EH18 ......60 C1
Well Ct EH4 ....62 B4
Wellington Pl EH6 ...16 C4
Wellington St EH7 ...16 B2
Wemyss Pl EH3 ......62 B4
Wemyss Pl Mews
EH3 ....62 B4

Werberside Mews
EH4 ....14 A4
West Adam St EH8 ...65 B2
West Annandale St
EH7 ....15 C3
West App Rd
Edinburgh EH1 ....24 B2
Edinburgh EH3 EH11 .63 A2
Westbank Loan EH15 .18 C1
Westbank Pl EH15 ...18 C1
Westbank St EH15 ...18 C1
West Bow
Edinburgh EH1 ....63 C2
Edinburgh EH1 ....65 A2
West Bowling Gn St
EH6 ....08 A1
West Brighton Cres
EH15 ....28 C4
West Bryson Rd
EH11 ....24 B1
Westburn Ave EH14 ..45 B4
Westburn Gr EH14 ...45 B4
Westburn Middlefield
EH14 ....45 B4
Westburn Pk EH14 ...45 C4
Westburn Prim Sch
EH11 ....33 C1
West Caystane Rd
EH10 ....48 C2
West Camus Rd
EH10 ....48 C2
West Carnethy Ave
EH13 ....46 C1
West Castle Rd EH10 .24 C1
West Catherine Pl
EH12 ....24 A3
West Cherrybank
EH6 ....07 B2
West Coates EH12 ...24 A3
West Colinton Ho
EH13 ....46 C2
West College St
EH12 ....65 A2
West Craigs Ave
EH12 ....20 B2
West Craigs Cres
EH12 ....20 B3
West Craigs Ind Est
EH12 ....20 B3
West Cromwell St
EH6 ....08 B2
West Crosscauseway
EH8 ....65 B1
West Ct
Edinburgh, Niddrie Mains
EH16 ....40 A3
Edinburgh, Ravelston
EH4 ....13 B1
West End Pl EH11 ....24 A1
Wester Broom Ave
EH12 ....21 B1
Wester Broom Dr
EH12 ....21 B1
Wester Broom Gdns
EH12 ....21 B1
Wester Broom Gr
EH12 ....21 B1
Wester Broom Pl
EH12 ....21 B1
Wester Broom Terr
EH12 ....21 B1
Wester Cl EH6 ....07 C3
Wester Coates Ave
EH12 ....24 A3
Wester Coates Gdns
EH12 ....24 A3
Wester Coates Pl
EH12 ....24 A3
Wester Coates Rd
EH12 ....24 A3
Wester Coates Terr
EH12 ....24 A3

Wester Drylaw Ave
EH4 ....13 A3
Wester Drylaw Dr
EH4 ....13 A3
Wester Drylaw Pk
EH4 ....13 B3
Wester Drylaw Pl
EH4 ....13 A3
Wester Drylaw Row
EH4 ....13 B2
Wester Hailes Ed Ctr
EH11 ....33 B1
Wester Hailes Pk
EH14 ....46 A4
Wester Hailes Rd
Edinburgh EH11 ......33 B2
Edinburgh EH14 ......45 C4
Wester Hailes Sta
EH14 ....45 C4
Wester Hill
Edinburgh EH10 ......36 A1
Edinburgh EH10 ......48 A4
Westerlea Sch EH12 ..23 B3
Western Gdns EH12 ..23 B3
Western General Hospl
EH4 ....13 C3
Western Pl EH12 .....23 B3
Western Terr EH12 ...23 B3
Wester Row EH14 ....32 A1
Wester Steil EH10 ...36 A1
West Ferry Field EH5 .06 B1
Westfield Ave EH11 ..23 B1
Westfield Rd EH11 ...23 C1
Westfield St EH11 ...23 C1
Westgarth Ave EH13 .47 A2
West Gorgie Pks 35 B4
West Gorgie Pl EH14 .35 B3
West Grange Gdns
EH9 ....37 C3
West Granton Access
EH4,EH5 ....05 C1
West Granton Rd
EH5 ....05 C2
Westhall Gdns EH10 ..25 A1
West Harbour Rd
EH5 ....06 A3
West Holmes Gdns
EH21 ....31 A2
Westland Cotts EH17 .52 A1
West Mains Rd EH9 ..38 B2
West Maitland St
EH12 ....63 A2
West Mayfield EH9 ...38 B4
West Mill Bank EH13 .46 C2
West Mill La EH4 ....62 A3
Westmill Rd EH10 ...60 C1
West Mill Rd EH13 ...46 B2
West Montgomery Pl B
EH7 ....16 B2
Westmost Cl EH6 ....07 B3
West Newington Pl
EH9 ....26 A1
West Nicolson St
EH8 ....65 B2
West Norton Pl EH7 ..64 C4
West Parliament Sq
EH1 ....64 A3
West Pilton Ave EH4 .13 B4
West Pilton Bank
EH4 ....05 A1
West Pilton Cres
EH4 ....05 A1
West Pilton Crossway
EH4 ....05 B1
West Pilton Dr EH4 ...05 B1
West Pilton Gdns
EH4 ....05 B1
West Pilton Gn EH4 ..05 B1
West Pilton Gr EH4 ..05 B1
West Pilton Lea EH4 .05 B1

West Pilton Loan
EH4 ....05 B1
West Pilton March
EH4 ....05 C2
West Pilton Pk EH4 ..05 B1
West Pilton Pl EH4 ...05 C1
West Pilton Rd EH4 ..05 C1
West Pilton Rise EH4 .05 A1
West Pilton Terr EH4 .05 B1
West Pilton View
EH4 ....13 B4
West Pk Pl EH11 .....24 B2
West Port EH1 ....63 C2
West Powburn EH9 ...38 A3
West Preston St EH8 .26 A1
West Register St
EH2 ....64 A4
West Register St La
EH2 ....64 A4
West Relugas Rd
EH9 ....37 C3
West Richmond St
EH8 ....65 B2
West Savile Rd EH16 .38 B3
West Savile Terr EH9 .38 A3
West Saville Gdns
EH9 ....38 B3
West Scotland St La B
EH3 ....15 B2
West Shore Bsns Ctr
EH5 ....5 B3
West Shore Rd EH5 ..05 B3
West Shore Rd Trad Est
EH5 ....5 B3
West Silvermills La
EH3 ....15 A2
West Telferton EH7 ..18 B1
West Tollcross EH3 ..63 B1
West Werberside
EH4 ....14 A4
West Winnelstrae
EH5 ....14 B4
West Woods EH4 .....14 A3
Wheatfield Loan
EH20 ....59 A1
Wheatfield Pl EH11 ..23 C1
Wheatfield Rd EH11 ..23 C1
Wheatfield St EH11 ..24 A1
Wheatfield Terr
EH11 ....23 C1
Whins Pl EH15 ....18 C1
Whitecraig Rd EH21 ..43 C1
Whitedales EH10 .....49 B1
Whitehall Ct EH4 ....13 A2
Whitehill Ave EH21 ..42 C4
Whitehill Farm Rd
EH21 ....42 C4
Whitehill Gdns EH21 .42 C4
Whitehill Rd EH15,
EH21, EH22 ....41 C3
Whitehill St EH21 ...41 C4
White Horse Cl EH8 ..64 C3
Whitehouse Loan
EH10 ....25 A1
Whitehouse Rd EH4 ..10 C4
Whitehouse Terr
EH9 ....37 B4
White Pk EH11 ......24 A1
Whitingford EH6 .....07 C1
Whitson Cres EH11 ..23 A1
Whitson Gr EH11 ....23 A1
Whitson Pl E EH11 ...23 A1
Whitson Pl W EH11 ..23 A1
Whitson Rd EH11 ....23 A1
Whitson Terr EH11 ...23 A1
Whitson Way EH11 ...23 A1
Whitson Wlk EH11 ...22 C1
Whyte Pl B EH7 .....16 C1

Wilfred Terr B EH8 ...17 B1
Williamfield Sq B
EH15 ....28 C4
William Jameson Pl
EH15 ....18 C1
William St EH3 ......62 A3
William St Ne La
EH3 ....62 A3
William St Nw La
EH3 ....62 A3
William St Se La EH3 .62 A3
William St Sw La 62 A3
Willowbank Row
EH6 ....07 C2
Willowbrae Ave EH8 ..27 B4
Willowbrae Gdns
EH8 ....27 C4
Willowbrae Rd
Edinburgh EH8 ....17 B1
Edinburgh EH8 ....27 C4
Willowpark (Spcl Sch)
EH11 ....23 C1
Wilson's Pk EH15 ....19 A1
Wilton Rd EH16 .....38 B2
Windmill La EH8 .....65 B1
Windmill St EH8 .....65 A1
Windsor Pl EH15 .....19 A2
Woodburn Terr EH10 .37 A3
Windsor St EH7 .....16 A2
Windsor St La EH7 ...16 A2
Winton Dr EH10 .....57 B4
Winton Gdns EH10 ...57 B4
Winton Gr EH10 .....49 A1
Winton Loan EH10 ...57 B4
Winton Pk EH10 .....57 A4
Winton Terr EH7 .....57 A4
Wishaw Terr EH7 ....17 A1
Wisp Gn EH15 ....41 A4
Wisp, The EH22 .....52 C4
Wolrige Rd EH16 ....52 A4
Wolseley Cres EH8 ..17 B1
Wolseley Terr EH8 ...17 B1
Woodbine Terr EH6 ..16 C3
Woodburn Terr EH10 .37 A3
Woodfield Ave EH13 .46 B2
Woodfield Pk EH13 ..46 B2
Woodhall Ave EH14 ..45 C2
Woodhall Bank EH13 .46 B1
Woodhall Dr EH14 ...45 C2
Woodhall Gr EH13 ...46 B1
Woodhall Millbrae
EH14 ....46 A2
Woodhall Rd
Edinburgh EH14 ......46 A2
Edinburgh EH1 ....46 C2
Woodhall Terr EH14 ..45 C2
Woodside Terr EH15 ..29 B3
Woodstock Pl EH16 ..39 A1
Woodville Terr EH6 ..16 C3
Woolmet Cres EH22 ..53 A4
Writer's Mus* EH1 ...64 A3
Wyvern Pk EH9 ......37 C4

Y/Z

Yardheads EH6 ....08 B1
Yeaman La EH11 .....24 B2
Yeaman Pl EH11 .....24 B2
Yewlands Cres EH16 .51 A3
Yewlands Gdns EH16 .51 A3
York La EH1 ....64 A4
York Pl EH1 ....64 A4
York Rd EH5 ....07 B2
Young St EH2 ....62 B3
Young St La N EH2 ..62 B4
Young St La S EH2 ..62 B3
Zetland Pl EH5 ......07 A2

List of numbered locations

n some busy areas of the maps it is not always
possible to show the name of every place.

Where not all names will fit, some smaller places are
shown by a number. If you wish to find out the
name associated with a number, use this listing.

*The places in this list are also listed normally in
the Index.*

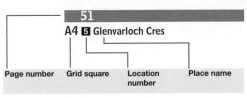

Page number   Grid square   Location
number   Place name

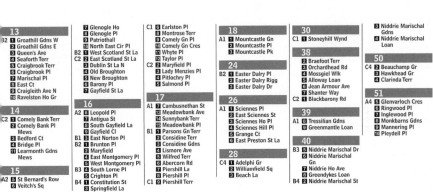

13

C2 **1** Groathill Gdns W
2 Groathill Gdns E
3 Queen's Ave
4 Seaforth Terr
5 Craigbrook Terr
6 Craigbrook Pl
7 Marischal Pl
8 East Ct
9 Craigleith Ave N
10 Ravelston Ho Gr

14

C2 **1** Comely Bank Terr
2 Comely Bank Pl
3 Bedford Ct
4 Bridge Pl
11 Learmonth Gdns
Mews

15

A2 **5** St Bernard's Row
6 Veitch's Sq

7 Glengle Ho
8 Glengle Pl
9 Patriothall
10 North East Cir Pl
B2 **1** West Scotland St La
C2 **2** East Scotland St La
3 Dublin St La N
4 Old Broughton
5 New Broughton
6 Barony Pl
7 Gayfield St La

16

A2 **6** Leopold Pl
7 Antigua St
8 South Gayfield La
9 Gayfield Cl
B1 **3** East Norton Pl
B2 **1** Brunton Pl
2 Maryfield
4 East Montgomery Pl
5 West Montgomery Pl
B3 **4** South Lorne Pl
5 Crighton Pl
B4 **1** Constitution St
3 Springfield La

C1 **6** Earlston Pl
7 Montrose Terr
8 Comely Gn Pl
9 Comely Gn Cres
11 Whyte Pl
12 Taylor Pl
C2 **2** Maryfield Pl
3 Lady Menzies Pl
4 Pitlochry Pl
5 Salmond Pl

17

A1 **7** Cambusnethan St
13 Meadowbank Ave
14 Sunnybank Terr
15 Meadowbank Pl
B1 **1** Parsons Gn Terr
2 Considine St
3 Considine Gdns
4 Lismore Ave
5 Wilfred Terr
6 Abercorn Rd
7 Piershill La
8 Piershill Pl
C1 **9** Piershill Terr

18

A1 **1** Mountcastle Gn
2 Mountcastle Pl
3 Mountcastle Pk

B2 **1** Easter Dalry Pl
2 Easter Dalry Rigg
3 Easter Dalry Dr

24

A1 **1** Sciennes Pl
2 East Sciennes St
3 Sciennes Ho Pl
4 Sciennes Hill Pl
5 Grange Ct
6 East Preston St La

28

C4 **1** Adelphi Gr
2 Williamfield Sq
3 Beach La

30

C1 **1** Stoneyhill Wynd

38

2 Braefoot Terr
3 Orchardhead Rd
4 Mossgiel Wlk
5 Alloway Loan
6 Jean Armour Ave
7 Shanter Way
C2 **1** Blackbarony Rd

39

A1 **8** Tressilian Gdns
9 Greenmantle Loan

40

B3 **5** Niddrie Marischal Dr
6 Niddrie Marischal
Gn
7 Niddrie Ho Ave
8 Greendykes Loan
B4 **2** Niddrie Marischal St

3 Niddrie Marischal
Gdns
4 Niddrie Marischal
Loan

50

C4 **2** Beauchamp Gr
3 Hawkhead Gr
4 Clarinda Terr

51

A4 **5** Glenvarloch Cres
6 Ringwood Pl
7 Inglewood Pl
8 Monkbarns Gdns
9 Mannering Pl
10 Pleydell Pl

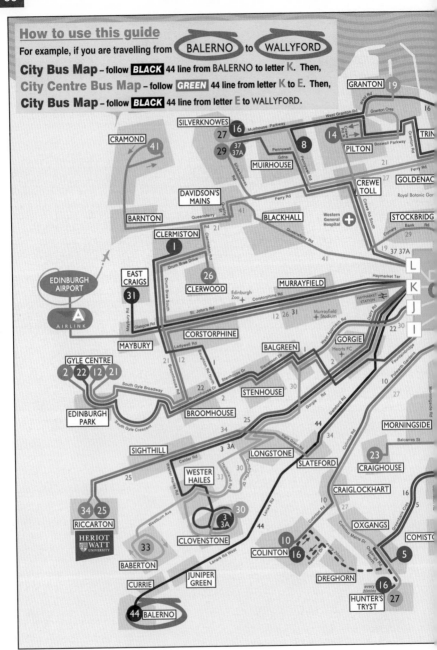

80

How to use this guide

For example, if you are travelling from **BALERNO** to **WALLYFORD**

City Bus Map – follow **BLACK** 44 line from BALERNO to letter **K**. Then,

City Centre Bus Map – follow **GREEN** 44 line from letter **K** to **E**. Then,

City Bus Map – follow **BLACK** 44 line from letter **E** to WALLYFORD.

GRANTON **19**

West Granton Rd · Granton Cres · **16**

SILVERKNOWES **16**
27 Muirhouse Parkway · West Granton Rd · **14** · TRIN

29 **37 37A** · Pennywell Gdns · **8** · PILTON · Boswall Parkway · Ferry Rd

MUIRHOUSE · Pennywell Rd · **21** · GOLDENAC

CRAMOND **41** · Ferry Rd · **27**

DAVIDSON'S MAINS · Queensferry Rd · CREWE TOLL · Royal Botanic Gar

BARNTON · Queensferry **41** · BLACKHALL · Western General Hospital · **+** · STOCKBRIDG · Bank Rd · Comely · **29**

CLERMISTON **1** · Queensferry Rd · **19** **37 37A**

Drum Brae Drive · **41**

EAST CRAIGS **31** · CLERWOOD **26** · MURRAYFIELD · Haymarket Ter · **L K J I**

EDINBURGH AIRPORT · **A** AIRLINK · Drum Brae South · Edinburgh Zoo · Corstorphine Rd · Murrayfield Stadium · HAYMARKET STATION · **22 30**

MAYBURY · Glasgow Rd · St. John's Rd · **12 26 31** · West Approach Rd · GORGIE · Hearts FC · Dalry Rd

CORSTORPHINE · Ladywell Rd · BALGREEN **1** · Gorgie Rd · **2**

GYLE CENTRE **2 22 12 21** · **21 12** · Broomhouse Rd · Stenhouse Dr · Stevenson Dr · **1** · STENHOUSE · **30** · Fountainbridge · Polwarth Gardens · **10** · **27**

EDINBURGH PARK · South Gyle Broadway · **22** · Broomhouse Dr · BROOMHOUSE · South Gyle Crescent · **25** · Inglis Green Rd · **44** · Slateford Rd · **34** · MORNINGSIDE · Morningside Rd · Balcarres St

SIGHTHILL · Calder Rd · **34** · **3 3A** · LONGSTONE · SLATEFORD · Colinton Rd · CRAIGHOUSE **23**

WESTER HAILES · Wester Hailes Rd · **33** · **30** · CRAIGLOCKHART · **16** · **5**

34 25 · Westburn Ave · **30** · **3 3A** · Lanark Rd · **10** · Colinton Rd · **27** · OXGANGS · Comiston Rd · COMISTO

RICCARTON · HERIOT WATT UNIVERSITY · **33** · CLOVENSTONE · **44** · Colinton Mains Dr · **5**

BABERTON · Lanark Rd West · COLINTON **10 16** · Redford Rd · DREGHORN · **16**

CURRIE · JUNIPER GREEN · HUNTER'S TRYST **27**

44 BALERNO

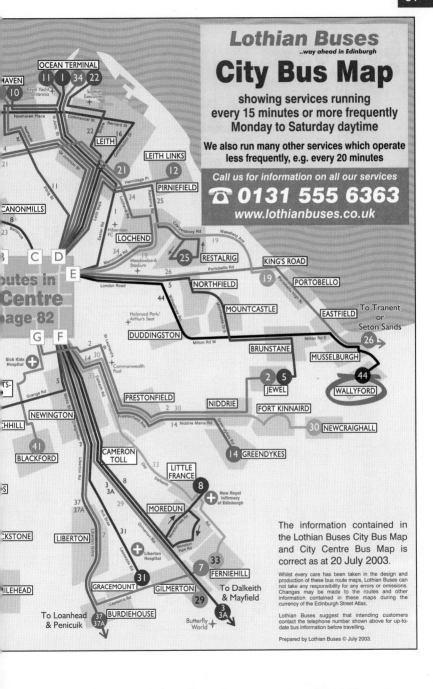

Lothian Buses
..way ahead in Edinburgh

City Bus Map

showing services running
every 15 minutes or more frequently
Monday to Saturday daytime

We also run many other services which operate
less frequently, e.g. every 20 minutes

Call us for information on all our services
☎ **0131 555 6363**
www.lothianbuses.co.uk

The information contained in
the Lothian Buses City Bus Map
and City Centre Bus Map is
correct as at 20 July 2003.

Whilst every care has been taken in the design and
production of these bus route maps, Lothian Buses can
not take any responsibility for any errors or omissions.
Changes may be made to the routes and other
information contained in these maps during the
currency of the Edinburgh Street Atlas.

Lothian Buses suggest that intending customers
contact the telephone number shown above for up-to-
date bus information before travelling.

Prepared by Lothian Buses © July 2003.

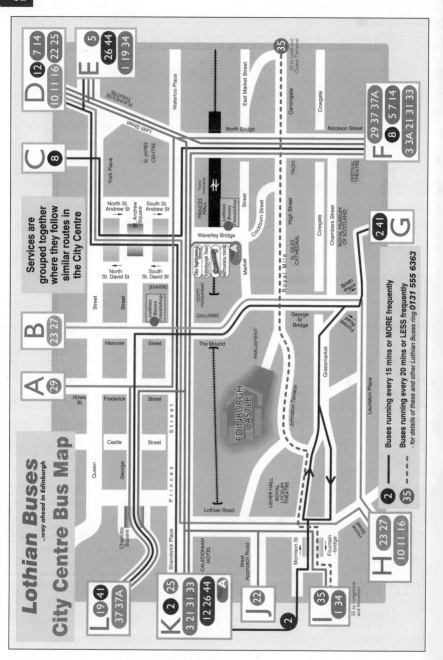